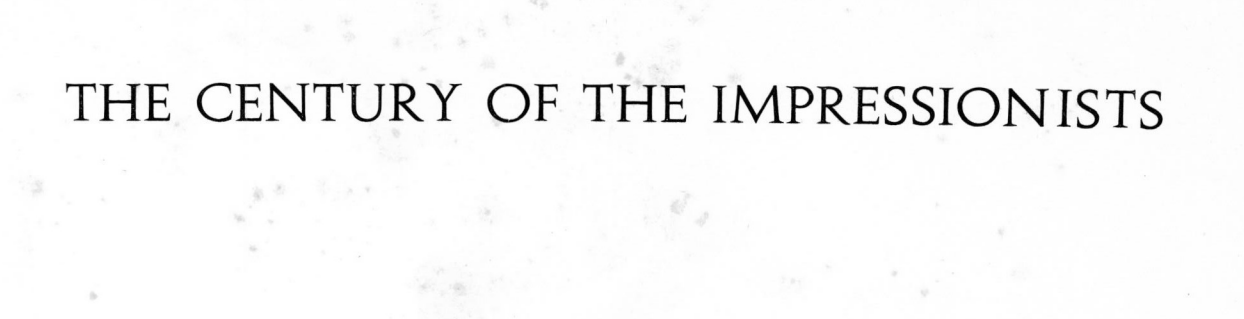

THE CENTURY OF THE IMPRESSIONISTS

THE CENTURY OF
THE IMPRESSIONISTS

BY

RAYMOND COGNIAT

CROWN PUBLISHERS INC. · NEW YORK

Translated by
GRAHAM SNELL

PRINTED IN ITALY – © 1978 BY BONFINI PRESS CORPORATION, NAEFELS, SWITZERLAND
ALL RIGHTS OF REPRODUCTION OF ILLUSTRATIONS BY S.P.A.D.E.M. AND A.D.A.G.P., PARIS
ALL RIGHTS IN THE U.S.A. RESERVED BY CROWN PUBLISHERS, INC., NEW YORK, N.Y.

William Turner   Venice. View of the « Piazzetta », c. 1840
Tate Gallery, London

THE FORERUNNERS · SUPREMACY OF SENTIMENT · THE ENGLISH LANDSCAPE-PAINTERS

The 19th century was a great century for French Art. David, Ingres and Delacroix made a deep impression on it, alternating the Classical and the Romantic. But profound as the effect of these geniuses may have been, the most significant event was Impressionism, not because of its exponents, who were perhaps no greater than the painters we have just mentioned, but because of its new way of thinking about painting. Previous conceptions were to be completely changed, and in their place one sees nothing less than the birth of Modern Art and a certain form of civilization.

The essential role given to the author of a work of art, and the independence of the artist with regard to the public – these belong essentially to the 19th century; they are a Romantic affirmation that proclaims the supremacy of the individual, even when he is opposed to the world that surrounds him. The Classical attitude is one of acceptance of the outside world, which enjoys the authority of a preconceived order.

Richard-Parkes Bonington Luxembourg Garden. c. 1820
Water-colour. British Museum, London

The liberation of thought could only be achieved at the price of an equivalent liberation of forms
and technique; it was produced concurrently in literature and in painting under the influence
of Romanticism, but it only takes on its true dimensions in the second half of the century, after
the last fierce defence of the methods that were believed, in spite of some abuse, to be the deposi-
taries of tradition. From that moment on, the famous definition of art – « Nature seen through
the eyes of the individual » – was justified.

This formula was certainly true in earlier times, but only adventitiously: the artist made a gift
of his personality as an addition to what he represented, the essential factor being the subject:
religious scene, battle, allegory or portrait.

The choice of subject – the first sign of liberation – modified the hierarchy of genres and transformed the social and moral preoccupations of the age. The Middle Ages had put the religious
theme first, ignoring landscape almost entirely, later giving it little by little a minor role. The
Renaissance attached less importance to the Sacred and more to Man, who assumed a divine
role through allegory. The 17th century saw the blooming of the historical picture; the 18th,
the greatest refinement in the portrait. In this movement towards the individual and a greater
familiarity with everyday life, landscape grew important in proportion with its increasing use
as a dramatic setting.

In this domain, as in others, the 18th century insisted on particularities and granted landscape
its independence. The Dutch, notably with Ruysdaël, played a major part in this development;
but it is primarily with the English, who advanced even further in the 19th century, that we
shall see landscape given a life of its own.

Constable is generally said to be the man responsible for this emancipation. But in his day and
before, a whole movement can be called to mind with John Crome, John Sell Cotman and
others; one could even go back to the 18th century with Gainsborough. They searched in the

6

open air for a liberty and, at the same time, an intimate contact with Nature, and these represent the beginnings of Romanticism much more than an individual achievement. The most original embodiment of these ideas is obviously the art of Constable. The French artists were all struck by it at an exhibition of English landscape-painters that was organized in Paris in 1824, and had a profound influence. Delacroix, it is said, was so troubled that he repainted the landscape « Massacre of Scio » in a few hours.

Constable, indeed, brought with him a spirit and technique whose novelty was bound to be particularly appealing to the Romanticists. He gave a sentimental undertone to a work of art, revealing the artist's temperament. Before him, the dramatic sentiment of a picture had been achieved through a background that was often theatrical and inevitably sacrificed the natural. In Constable, Nature is not arranged; it is observed and reproduced so as to bring out certain distinctive features. The technique lends it a new expressive meaning: the light touch seems to scratch the picture, not trying to follow the form of the object; it is like a modulation of the atmosphere; space is suggested less by the drawing and perspective than by the colour; a sort of sensuality shakes itself free from the solid world with the urgency of a lyrical appeal.

Another English painter, Turner, played an even greater role in extolling the poetry of light; given new life by him, it bursts in fairy scenes, dissolves forms, transforms landscape into iridescent, moving vapours, so that an intense, shifting life surges out of the mist. Time was when Ruysdaël or Watteau had been able to show foliage bathed in sunlight; Turner went further. He was not content to observe, being himself at the very centre of this luminosity, this whirl of fire,

William Turner   Calm Weather. 1809
Etching. British Museum, London

John Constable Trees. 1817 Etching. Bibliothèque Nationale, Paris

Honoré-Victorin Daumier Return from Market. c 1870 Oscar Reinhart Collection, Winterthur, Switzerland

10   *Edouard Manet* The Fifer. 1866 Musée du Louvre, Paris

Jean-Baptiste-Camille Corot   Girl with Red Sweater. 1845-50   Emil G. Buehrle Collection, Zurich

Jean-Baptiste-Camille Corot Landscape. Castelgandolfo. c. 1870
Musée du Louvre, Paris

Jean-Baptiste-Camille Corot Trees. c. 1852 Pen-and-ink drawing. Musée des Beaux-Arts, Lille

Honoré Daumier The Sick Man. c. 1849
Water-colour and pen-and-ink drawing. E. Rouart Collection, Paris

this explosion that spreads on all sides. The real world loses all solidity and density; it is the moment of the sumptuous, elementary fusion in which the fantastic emerges. The art of Turner was a prelude to that of Monet.

Bonington actually lived in France and his influence was to be more immediate. Without losing himself in the reveries of Turner, he found a wealth of unexplored themes in the everyday scene. Above all, he looked at the sky with keen sensibility, he revealed the clouds with their infinite variety of forms and nuances, their unceasing life. He loved their clear, shadowless tonalities. He anticipated Jongkind and, above all, Boudin.

There is an obvious foreshadowing of Impressionism in all these English painters; they announce the enrichment of vision through the direct observation of Nature – even when they idealise it – and a desire to render the instability of atmosphere, to freeze movement without destroying it. The development of the water–colour technique in England in the 18th century also encouraged this taste for rapid execution. And this was to be one of the preoccupations of Impressionism.

THE SUPREMACY OF NATURE

THE FRENCH LANDSCAPE-PAINTERS

The importance given to landscape in the 19th century by the English, and the example also given by Holland with Ruysdaël, Hobbema and others in the preceding century, were to be echoed in the French painters. Several of these, reacting against Academic disciplines, drew near to Nature and, thinking that landscape observed on the spot offered more vital lessons than work in a studio, installed themselves in Barbizon.

Honoré Daumier The Lawyers. Study. c. 1850
Water-colour and pen-and-ink drawing. Private Collection, Paris

By a curious coincidence, we already find a « Fontainebleau School » at the birth of French Classicism during the Renaissance, and a new « Fontainebleau School » – but of a quite different kind – marked the first stage of a fundamental change in French painting at the beginning of the 19th century. Théodore Rousseau, Diaz, Harpignies and Daubigny were the most brilliant examples of it. Théodore Rousseau had been especially attracted by trees, by their majesty as much as by their structure. Before Cézanne, he sought to express what was strong and lasting in them, to show how they lent landscape a stable solidity while other plants suggested movement and change. The fine oaks of Théodore Rousseau anticipate the role that Cézanne was to make pines play in the construction of a picture although Cézanne preferred the skeleton of trees and Rousseau their mass, to which he gave a physical density. In Cézanne they have the same plastic quality, the same human presence, as people in the earlier historical pictures have. Some are like portraits, with the marks of personality, the beauty and the blemishes, that make up an individual. Diaz is nearer Constable, more romantic; in the intensity of plant life, he shows the depths of the forests where sombre lights gleam.

Daubigny was nearer the Impressionists, who were to follow. He painted country scenes with wide, distant horizons, and vast watery skies. He painted the transparence of the air, subtleties of light or turbid greys.

Harpignies was still more detached from the past. He was like an artisan, a calm and scrupulous observer – as Sisley was to be; he did not try to astonish, but the sureness he brought to observation and execution would have made him a great painter, if only he had had some genius.

Claude Monet   Portrait of Camille Monet. 1866-7
Red-chalk drawing. Private Collection, New York

16

Constantin Guys Two Girls in a Theatre Box
Albertina Collection, Vienna

17

Gustave Courbet The Stone Breakers. c. 1870 Gemäldegalerie, Dresden

Edouard Manet   Lunch in the Studio. 1868   Bayerische Staatsgemälde Collection, Munich

Jean Frédéric Bazille Family Gathering. 1866
Musée du Louvre, Paris

Constantin Guys A Lady of Fashion, 1860
Water-colour. Phillips Memorial Gallery, Washington, D.C.

Jean-Baptiste-Camille Corot Study of Trees
Crayon drawing. Private Collection, Paris

22

Jean-Baptiste-Camille Corot The Horseman in the Woods
Stereotype-plate

23

But he was no more than a minor master who subscribed to the evolution started at the beginning of the century, and so proves how inevitable the growth of the new ideas was, since they did not only stem from the greatest.

In all these paintings, people are in little evidence and often even absent; the artist's sentiments imbue the work and do not need the support of anecdote; the picture increasingly rejects storytelling and becomes its own raison d'être. This conquest, which the Impressionists were to carry further, was to become the chief pretext for a scandal; but there was no suspicion then of the consequences of this revolution. The real meaning of things is always known too late, when the future has made it obvious and nothing can be altered.

Théodore Rousseau was certainly to know the hostility of the defenders of Academicism for some years, but this was no longer to prevail after 1849.

Corot, who belonged to the same generation and bound himself very closely to the School of Fontainebleau, could trouble no one with his art of refinement, so rare and tasteful. He was more in the Vernet tradition than in that of Ruysdaël and nourished himself, moreover, at the most Classical sources, in Italy and especially in the Roman countryside, from which he brought back landscapes of a simple grandeur. For those who like comfortable traditional explanations, let us say that he served as a link between Poussin and Cézanne; but it was to be a long time before it became evident.

This is the place to notice the role Corot gave to light, a light that never dramatises the landscape,

Jean-François-Millet The Tramps
Black-lead drawing. Corcoran Gallery of Art, Washington, D.C.

but lends it a calm that Cézanne was to try to achieve by other methods.

With the desire to capture the atmosphere of a place, Corot studied the Impressionists' methods but, at the same time, opposed them by retaining the permanent values and creating Classical compositions, sometimes even going so far as to add or displace motifs – trees or houses – to obtain a better-organized harmony. But the Impressionists were to try to reproduce Nature as it is, in her most fleeting changes. Thus Corot points to the reactionary Cézanne and the subsequent return to Classicism, to which several movements subscribed, from Cubism onwards. The pictures painted in the vicinity of Paris are less strictly Classical than those inspired by Italy – and perhaps one should recognize in his vaporous evocations of Ville d'Avray a prelude to the mists of Claude Monet – but in him the concern for truth does not go as far as Realism.

Unlike the other Fontainebleau painters, Corot did not devote himself exclusively to landscape. He gave an important place to the human figure and, if his portraits were scarcely appreciated in his lifetime, they are considered today one of the greatest contributions of the 19th century. Here again, Corot served as a link between the past and the future. There are plenty of portraits – and very true to life, one senses. Yet they are treated without concessions, with the same calm observation that Cézanne was to carry to its ultimate extreme, to the point of considering the human face with the same placid indifference as a still life; did he not say to his mother: « I should like you to pose like an apple »?

Corot's characters herald this calm lucidity. Corot's life and its origins, point to the art that was to develop. His background (he belonged to the comfortable petite bourgeoisie), his modest needs and prudent, rather unambitious existence – even when he was successful – show that a new social class had been established. It illustrates a movement towards the foundation of a harmonious middle way in life – not necessarily mediocre, however; excesses were put aside *a priori* but accepted when they became inevitable or necessary, because it was decided that the movement should achieve its destiny peacefully, and realise its aims in suitable forms, which it itself elaborated. One must bear these ideas in mind if one wants to understand the nature of those who made Impressionism, and be able to see below the surface of their work.

THE PASSION FOR LIBERTY: THE SUPREMACY OF MAN

DAUMIER, GUYS, COURBET, MILLET

The active revolutionary role was to be taken up by others, for the chief event of the 19th century, and one that was bound to have consequences for art, was the discovery of individual liberty. « Do what you please, as you please » was a new principle for the painter who, no longer bound by the order and rules of the Academicians, renounced official art and set off on a discovery of himself. Romanticism and its sequel, Realism, were the result of this new state of affairs. Man is given pride of place, be it in Romanticism through exaltation, or in Realism through the wish to know him better and accept his defects and qualities – the two sides of a single ambition. Romanticism was an amplification: Realism the reaction against it; but both set themselves the same goal: to present a true image of life. Delacroix would have liked to be able to draw a person while he was falling from the fifth floor – the photographic reporter's dream. Daumier found in the street, in the Law Courts, and in Parliament, some most extraordinary models for his cruel humanity; Courbet coldly watched a funeral procession at Ornans. They were all scrupulous slaves of truth and, for fear of softening it, were often tempted to exaggerate it.

Edouard Manet Nude Study. 1864
Water-colour. Knoedler Gallery, New York

From that moment on, the whole century was to be marked by this desire to catch things on the run. The painter was inspired by a documentary Realism which was to become ever more evident and of which Constantin Guys gives us a foretaste. His topical drawings were actually done for newspapers; they are marked by that rapid observation and execution, by that characteristic detailed precision, by the sense of movement, so widespread in the 19th century. One can find the prelude to all this in the 18th century, notably in the discerning notes of Saint-Aubin, which predict this new role of painter-reporter.

Photography, discovered at just the right moment to quicken this current of ideas, put a mechanical process at its disposal; at the same time, it liberated painting from the imitation of the real and, doing this, forced it to look both for other subjects and other methods than those accepted up to then. In fact, since photography freezes the moment so completely and suddenly that it renders the person and the object inert, the painter understood that his role was not to compete with an instrument, but, on the contrary, to capture life and its throb in each frozen instant.

At this time, technique took on a supreme importance because it became clear that the artist went beyond the simple reproduction of Nature. The lightning flash of Daumier the painter links Manet with Fragonard, just as Courbet's nudes make way for Renoir's; and as their free composition was to be a justification for that of the Impressionists, so the difficulties they posed were to make those of Impressionism acceptable. Here, in fact, begins the conflict between the public and the artist – and even more between the *Institut*, congealed in its academics, and living art.

26

Frédéric Bazille Manet Drawing. 1869
Charcoal drawing. Marc Bazille Collection, Montpellier

Henri-Théodore Fantin-Latour Self-Portrait
Charcoal. Musée des Beaux-Arts, Lille

A conflict that was to last nearly a century – and one cannot say that it is over today.
Millet was to play an intermediary role between the School of Fontainebleau and the Realists.
A large part of his work was done at Barbizon and testifies to the same love of the forest that
Théodore Rousseau evinces; but with his peasants and his free technique, notably in the por-
traits, he was nearer Courbet. His humility, his troubled, toilsome life, almost like an artisan's,
and his death in poverty – these place him beside Daumier.
Courbet, Daumier and Millet represent both a new technique and a new social outlook: their
attitude – resigned in Millet, militant in the other two – reflects the same desire to accomplish an
individual destiny, even if it did not conform to accepted rules.
One often strives to find a sign of this independence in the lives of these artists, rather than in

Eugène Boudin The Beach at Trouville. 1863
Ittleson Collection, New York

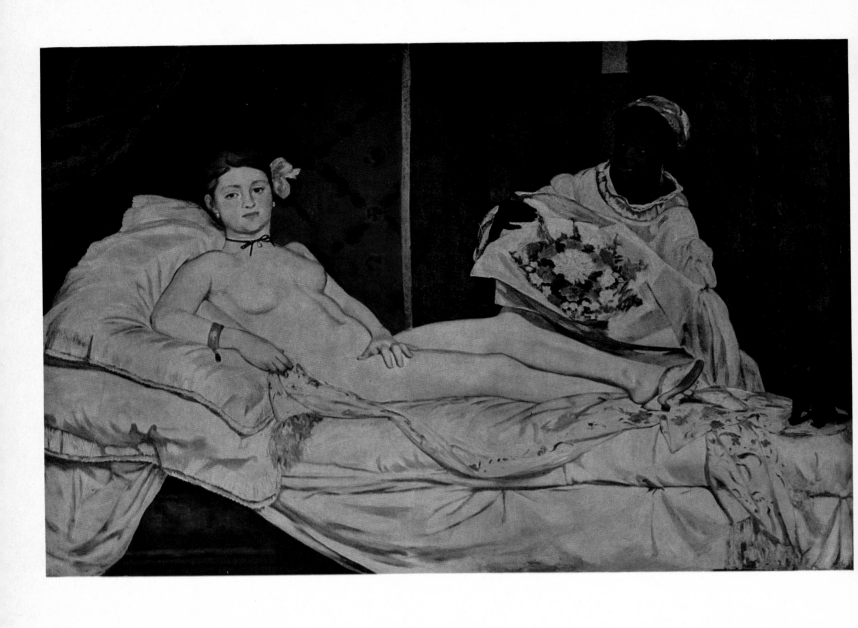

Edouard Manet Olympia. 1863
Musée du Louvre, Paris

30

Edouard Manet Déjeuner sur l'Herbe (The Picnic). 1863
Musée du Louvre, Paris

Pierre-Auguste Renoir Portrait of Sisley. 1868
Emil G. Buehrle Collection, Zurich

33

◁ *Pierre-Auguste Renoir* Mademoiselle Sicot. 1865
National Gallery, Chester Dale Collection, Washington D.C.

Edgar Degas Portrait of a Young Woman. 1867
Musée du Louvre, Paris

Claude Monet Madame Gaudibert. 1868 ▷
Musée du Louvre, Paris

Edouard Manet Portrait of Emile Zola. 1868
Musée du Louvre, Paris

Edouard Manet The Reading. 1868
Musée du Louvre, Paris

Claude Monet La Grenouillère. 1869 Metropolitan Museum of Art, New York

Claude Monet Boats at Argenteuil. 1874 Durand-Ruel Collection, Paris

Claude Monet « Impression-Rising Sun ». 1872
Musée Marmottan, Paris

40

their technique, although this is no less significant. Of course, in his political caricatures Daumier took up a standpoint that the government thought it could answer with prohibitions, penalties and even imprisonment; but his brush-stroke, which heavily strikes the canvas, is also provocative. In the subjects chosen by Courbet, in his aims, in his exhibitions (such as the one organised in a hovel at the gate of the 1855 Exhibition from which he had been turned away) a constant protest is evident. Yet what shocked his contemporaries even more was his rejection of academic conventions. His models were friends or lively-looking girls, human beings and not idealistic divinities. So much so that the Empress Eugène cannot conceal her irritation with the powerful peasant women and is about to strike one of the bathers with her riding whip, to treat her like a « Percheron » – bathers who, at a *Salon*, made a scandalous contrast with the syrupy Venuses that were then the rage. Millet represented peasants at their work, in their humble life, without romanticising them at all; and this simple image was also a piece of bravado, since it was hardly to the taste of a society used to brilliant receptions, to the artificial glitter of luxury, a society in which art was willingly accepted – on condition that it did not take the form of social protest.

But all that is too earnest, too weighty; everyone knows that the artist became a living protest, that he was calling for a world different from that which prevailed. It was an ideology that took humanity, held down before, into account; and it showed some recognition of the rights of the individual.

The subjects of the pictures surprised, sometimes irritated, but people did not yet dare to rave against the technique, since they did not appreciate its telling power.

These material facts appear very significant to us today, and proclaim a future completely

Johann Barthold Jongkind   The Port of Honfleur. 1865
Water-colour. Petit Palais, Paris

Eugène Boudin   Women on a Beach. 1863
Water-colour. Petit Palais, Paris

different from the past. The *Salon des Refusés* of 1863 was the last sign before the break, or perhaps the first sign of the break itself.

As early as 1848, after the revolutionary days, the organization of a *Salon* without a selection committee, had revealed the stirrings of independence; but the scant success of this event, and the mediocrity of the pictures shown, had finally proved a set-back to the partisans of liberty. Official Art, although losing a little more ground every day, believed it was still strong enough to fight against the new ideas. After having been indifferent, it showed itself more and more rigid, and its outright refusals finally gave its victims an opportunity to protest. The affair grew big enough for the Emperor to allow the setting-up of the *Salon des Refusés*, where there were to figure some of the painters who, in after years, became the glory of French Art.

THE PRE-IMPRESSIONISTS

At this time, Impressionism was already born, but no one yet knew it: it had not received its baptism. Who would have dreamt that a few stray youngsters would unite under one banner. At the very most, one might have discerned a movement in favour of luminous painting and protested at the independence of a Manet, whose scandalous attitude was linked to that of Courbet. His case, moreover, appeared much graver since he belonged to the *haute bourgeoisie* – the very class that showed itself hostile to the new ideas. His art was a denial, a betrayal of his social class.

42

Today we misunderstand the anger sparked off by the showing of « Déjeuner sur l'herbe » in 1863, at the *Salon des Refusés*, and by « Olympia » in 1865. Above all, we do not understand how they could violently attack such traditional subjects and see, in both of them, an offence against morality, while without offending anyone, the museums and even the *Salons* of that time were showing Venuses, Junos and Dianas, as scantily clad as were Manet's models, who were a naked young woman with some men in everyday dress, and another no less naked in a bedroom – but without any mythological pretext.

In fact, although they would not admit it, the technique disconcerted them as much as the subject did. Until then, they had considered that a work of art should be a creation of the spirit, and the product of the studio; Nature was reconsidered in it, recontrived. Even the landscape-painters we have mentioned in the preceding pages had not fundamentally changed this conception.

The art of Manet represents a sharp break. Fresh air enters the landscape. The young people in « Déjeuner sur l'herbe » are those one meets in life; the woman sitting among them has just undressed and none of them wants to make believe that they are gods. Proceeding from this obvious fact (since « Olympia » does not pretend to Greek divinity either), she could only be a street girl exhibiting herself on a couch, and thus unacceptable to bourgeois dignity, even if the artist was inspired by her to the Venus of a Titian, even if, in « Déjeuner sur l'herbe », he recaptured the composition of a Raphael.

In fact, Manet, the alleged revolutionary, so respected Classical tradition that, several times, he openly made use of old masterpieces; yet no one thought of considering his kinship, not even of uncovering it.

Constantin Guys   The Carriage. c. 1870
Water-colour and pen-and-ink drawing. Phillips Memorial Gallery, Washington, D.C.

Alfred Sisley July 14th at Daybreak. 1878
Pen-and-ink drawing. Private Collection, New York

Similar observations could be made concerning colour: that brilliant, glossy paint, spread wide; the noble beauty of those greys, the elegance of those blacks – they could have been found in Goya or Velasquez, for Manet never concealed his taste for Spanish painting. But because tradition came to life again through him and was not mewed up by scholastic schlerosis, it was a scandal.

The bourgeois conformist, tied to his social milieu, and wishing to go on showing his work in the *Salons*, in spite of the malevolence and the refusals that he had to face, was so little of a rebel that he would not even take part in the exhibitions of Impressionist painters, of which however he was the initiator. This discreet Frenchman who, at the end of his life, was to rejoice in receiving the *Légion d'Honneur* – thanks to the faithfulness of a friend, Antonin Proust, who had become a Cabinet Minister – appeared a rebel in spite of himself and was never wholly to appease his adversaries. At the time of his greatest successes, and even after his death, he was to go on stirring up passionate disputes; for the entry into the national museums of that incontestable masterpiece, « Olympia », was only possible through an open subscription among the public and on the insistence of Georges Clémenceau, a powerful politician, and an admirer of Manet's, who imposed his will against the wishes of officials.

Such blindness proves what deeply-rooted prejudices the Impressionists were to have to overcome. Their movement could not have triumphed through individuals; collective action was necessary to group the artists and their supporters together.

If Manet can be considered the leader round whom the newcomers were soon to rally, he was not the only one to have prepared for their arrival. It is true, though, that the art of Boudin or of Jongkind was much more discreet and could not lead to such vehement debates.

44

These artists gave a foretaste of the future in their landscapes, be it the Seine Valley with Boudin, or Holland with Jongkind. Landscapes of pearly grisailles, of vast skies that join up with the earth – or the sea – towards a far horizon.

Never had such care been taken to suggest atmosphere. In certain of their works, the landscape itself hardly counts any more; in Boudin it only binds the clouds and the waves together, in highly refined tones, in moving, shadowy forms, which answer one another. At most, a narrow strip of beach in the foreground, welcomes some people who are also painted in flowing daubs and have hardly any more consistency than the sea or the sky; they are placed there as if to set off this soft fairyland. Some of Turner's or Bonington's studies could have given a preview of this development, but they were only notes for other compositions; with Boudin, these sketches become the goal to be attained; they are the work of art.

In Jongkind, there are no people at all. The wide Dutch countryside stretches as far as the eye can see, to an horizon that bulges gently and rhythmically with the spidery silhouette of a windmill or the mast of some barge.

In both, Nature lives in a great calm, which does not lack movement; in a great silence, which is not oppressive, where the air is moist, as during rainbows.

Boudin and Jongkind were naturally to figure among the Impressionists and take part in their first exhibitions since, several years before them, they had discovered the source of inspiration and liberation that landscape is, and because they too understood the forgotten possibilities of luminous colours.

Camille Pissarro Pontoise. 1873
Pen-and-ink drawing. Mallet Collection, Paris

Charles-François Daubigny Fishing in Springtime. 1870
Pen-and-ink drawing. Musée du Louvre, Paris

THE FIRST GENERATION

THE PAINTERS OF FLEETING CHANGE

All the forerunners we have just enumerated banded together little by little and we can understand today that, in these circumstances, revolution was inevitable.

Claude Monet was the one who, of them all, most completely epitomised the ideas and works that were to be grouped under the Impressionist banner; only in him could the whole history of the movement be summarised.

Through his family, he belonged to that careful petite bourgeoisie who do not see their children embark on an artistic career without some disquiet. He lived his childhood years at Le Havre; that is, among those coastal scenes, in that Seine Valley which inspired the forerunners and was to be the favourite spot for all the Impressionists; and under those tender grey skies, among those verdant fields, was born a connoisseur of light. How well he knew the soft fairylands that Nature offered him from day to day! A refugee in London during the 1870 War, he discovered in Turner all that a painter can achieve from this inspiration and from the marvellous effects of light. After the war, he met his friends, Renoir and Sisley, in Paris again – friends he had known in Gleyre's studio. But Bazille, the one who had given proof of the rarest qualities, was – alas –

46

missing; he had joined the Zouaves and had been killed in 1870.

Contacts were renewed between those who had been meeting on Friday evenings at the Café Guerbois, 9 avenue de Clichy, since 1866, and had been passionately defending Manet's ideas. When, on April 15th, 1874, the first exhibition of the « Anonymous Society of Painters, Sculptors and Engravers » was opened by the photographer, Nadar, in a rented room on the first floor of 35 boulevard des Capucines, they did not imagine they were participating in an historic event, but listened to protests against the embargo imposed by the official selection committee. A violent storm burst immediately. Claude Monet was to be the pretext because he had shown a picture entitled: « Impression. Rising Sun ». Louis Leroy, the editor of « Charivari », found a fine caption on which to hang his irony and, scorning the young painters who were so little concerned to follow the beaten track, he described them as *Impressionists*. The epithet enjoyed such success that, some years later, those concerned adopted it themselves.

We have to admit today that the title given by Monet to his picture was as provocative as the painting, and completely upset long-acknowledged ideas. In writing « Impression » in the catalogue, Claude Monet affirmed, no doubt unconsciously, the artist's desire to make his personality prevail; for him, the subject had become secondary and the essential factor was his own feeling. It was not necessary to give landscape precise contours, since placing the scene mattered little. This one title thus sufficed to point out the way that was followed for some years. The artist had formerly been a superior artisan, obedient to commands, compelled to satisfy public taste, treating the well-defined subject that was expected of him. From then on, the artist gave priority to his own emotion and publicly testified to his state of mind, asking people to understand him: the work of art became a confidence and, with his title, Claude Monet said so with a frankness that was deemed inadmissible.

At the same time, these artists adopted a very free way of painting, which well suited their

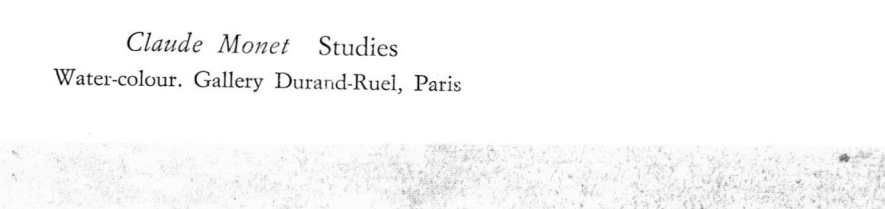

Claude Monet Studies
Water-colour. Gallery Durand-Ruel, Paris

new way of thinking. They tried to preserve in the finished painting the spontaneous quality of a sketch, to catch the fleetingness of the moment, of life in the open air; they had recourse to quick outlines and did not try to hide the freshness of their improvisations– far from it. Doing this, they aroused the scorn and anger of the right–thinking academic, who loves unadventurous, careful work done in a studio.

The situation grew worse in the following years. On the occasion of the sale that these same artists organised at the Hôtel Drouot, on 24th March 1875, the critics were even harsher. The most violent attacks, however, did not induce the painters to climb down, so completely did they believe in the ideas and techniques they were defending. The inevitable evolutions that followed were not to succeed in shaking these artists' convictions.

As far as Monet was concerned, this affirmation was to be increasingly free of all constraint. No one could better reproduce living light and the fleeting changes it produces in the appearance of things.

Like him, his friends, Sisley and Pissarro, applied themselves to preserving the image of quivering life, the shimmering of water or foliage. Manet, to whom they referred in their apologia for luminous colour, was not to take part in their group exhibitions, but was to submit in his turn to their influence and give light to his palette.

A young woman, Berthe Morisot, was to bring a very personal element of tenderness and elegance into the group, which had its source in both Manet and the landscape-painters.

These painters can be considered the kernel of Impressionism, as the most faithful followers of the doctrine evolved under this banner.

Claude Monet The Port of Touques. 1865
Black-stone drawing. Private Collection, New York

Camille Pissarro The Approach to the Village. 1872
Musée du Louvre, Paris

Camille Pissarro The Road to Louveciennes. 1870
Musée du Louvre, Paris

50

Alfred Sisley The Canal. 1872
Musée du Louvre, Paris

Camille Pissarro The Harvest. 1876 Musée du Louvre, Paris

Charles-François Daubigny The Cliffs of Villerville. 1864 Black-stone drawing. Private Collection, Lausanne

There is a hidden contradiction in their art: they observed reality with precision in order to extract the poetry of everyday life from it, and yet froze movement, the moment, in order to fix what was temporary. They saw only colour, air, and water in the most solid landscape, even that of a city; and yet they respected its reality. They used only luminous colours, without contrasts of dark shadows, in order to suggest brilliant sunshine. Never had the intimate exploration of Nature gone so far. The Impressionist landscape is like a portrait – it reveals Nature's state of mind.

The scientific explanations that have been given for the birth of Impressionism in connection with the discoveries of physicists such as Chevreul, Helmolz and others, are superficial; the

Pierre-Auguste Renoir Repose. 1880
Black-lead. The Art Institute of Chicago

Edgar Degas Portrait of Marguerite Degas.   Crayon drawing. Musée du Louvre, Paris

Johann Barthold Jongkind The Port of Anvers. Setting Sun Etching

Adolphe Monticelli Oriental Scene. 1876 Musée des Beaux Arts, Algiers

Pierre-Auguste Renoir The Reader. 1874-76
Musée du Louvre, Paris

Edouard Manet The Sultana. 1871
Emil G. Buehrle Collection, Zurich

Edgar Degas Count Napoléon Lepic with his Children. 1871
Emil G. Buehrle Collection, Zurich

Pierre-Auguste Renoir Maternity. 1885
Red-chalk drawing. Private Collection, London

Pierre-Auguste Renoir Dancing at Bougival. 1883
Crayon drawing. Private Collection, New York

Jean-Louis Forain In the Restaurant
Lithograph

invention or intuition of the painters counted far more than their knowledge of the physical laws governing light.

What remains certain is that, while Impressionism was the work of a number of powerful individuals, it suited a time when profound changes, social, intellectual and scientific, occurred; a time when the principal of the creator asserting his rights over the mass was modifying the structure of society, when the rhythm of life made rapid changes preferable to steady evolution, when sensation and visual reality were becoming more convincing than demonstration by reasoning. To these new ways of living and thinking, Impressionism responded immediately; and the ideas that it advanced were, with their originality, inevitably shocking to the majority of a public as yet unaware of the changes that surrounded it.

The art of Monet, Sisley and Pissarro takes on the appearance of improvisation, which was necessary to the ephemeral aspect they sought to reproduce. It was obviously in contradiction with the idea – to which people had been accustomed – of Art in its workmanlike perfection, in its meticulous application of a craft – for which the modern artists substituted intensity and inspiration. The accuracy and rapidity of their observation were matched by rapidity and accuracy of execution.

However, besides those who were exclusively landscape-painters, other artists, all really belonging to the group, all taking part in its exhibitions, had rather different aspirations and temperaments. Renoir, Degas and Cézanne were among those who did not submit strictly to the rules, to such an extent that many historians have tried to detach them from Impressionism. This would be very unfair and inaccurate, since those concerned never pushed their disagreement to such a point, and for years participated in the common fight; but their nature carried them towards other forms, towards more stable expressions than those of the landscape-painters.

Degas, for example, never dreamed of severing his links with the Classical tradition. But, since this was dying because of the narrowness of an academic dictatorship, he joined the revolutionaries' clan and threw himself into the struggle – that is to say, into what was alive. Apart from this rebellious attitude, everything should have turned him away from Impressionism: in his technique he did not adopt the short detached stroke; even later when, in his pastels, he used shading lines, he did not seek the mobility of the landscape-painters at all. His drawing traces the contours of each object with passion. Among his subjects, landscapes are extremely rare and always secondary, so that the chief place in them, in contrast with the painters mentioned earlier, is given to the human being. Even the spirit that animates his work is different: in Degas one senses an almost dispassionate observer, while in the others there shines a luminous *joie de vivre*. He is the image of introspection: they of expansion. He retained something of Ingres,

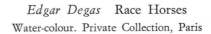

Edgar Degas   Race Horses
Water-colour. Private Collection, Paris

Edgar Degas Before the « Take Off », 1883
National Museum, Ottawa, Canada

Camille Pissarro The Orchard. 1877
Musée du Louvre, Paris

66

Alfred Sisley The Boat during the Flood. 1876
Musée du Louvre, Paris

Edouard Manet Monet Painting on the Seine. 1874
Bayerische Staatsgemälde Collection, Munich

69

Alfred Sisley The Bridge at Argenteuil, 1872
Ittleson Collection, New York

Ittleson Collection, New York

Berthe Morisot The Balcony. 1872
Ittleson Collection, New York

Claude Monet Jean Monet in his Cradle. 1867 ▷
Mr. and Mrs. George Friedland's Collection, Merion, Pennsylvania

Pierre-Auguste Renoir   Young Man in the Forest of Fontainebleau. 1886   Museum of Sao Paulo, Brasil

whose pupil he was; something austere, that never lets itself go, even when he painted dancers in brilliant costumes under blazing footlights.

Degas' work, moreover, rarely evokes the open air; he preferred to work in indoor light – studio, theatre or other places – where he could paint forms and lighting, confirming there again his fidelity to a tradition with which he nevertheless believed he had broken.

Thus, Degas established the connection between the past and Impressionism. He was attached to Impressionism because of his chosen theme in life, the authentic documentation of the present; because of his use of fresh colours, his independent attitude, and his rejection of sterile conventions. Moreover, he belonged to Impressionism, both because he was to figure in several of the group's exhibitions, notably in the first, and because he came in for his share of criticism. But at the same time he belonged to the past through the great respect he always retained for learning, through his love of drawing, through the patient finish he put into his work, and through his refusal to accept the chance result.

Opposed to Degas, we find Cézanne. He was also in the Impressionist movement, rather as an outsider who was to go his way when he had no more to get out of it. But, while Degas was a half-open door to the past, Cézanne was a wide-open door to the future; it was to him that all the progressive artists were to refer in the 20th century. He was nearer Impressionism than Degas was, and was seriously influenced by it during his stays in Paris and the surrounding region. He was close to the movement also because of his taste for landscape and the liberty he found in it; and because of his break with the past in his search for an individual technique – although, like Degas, he rejected what was of only temporary value.

He sought what was lasting and set aside all sentimentality, so as to consider only the plastic quality of a subject. He observed and analysed a landscape, a woman, or a fruit-dish with the same calm lucidity. Very judiciously, he could say: « I should have liked to make Impressionism a solid, lasting thing, like museum art. » The museum for which Cézanne worked was the museum of tomorrow, while with Degas it was that of yesterday; but both of them tended to extend the movement to which they belonged, stretching it beyond its immediate limits, beyond the simple feeling so admirably summed up by Monet.

Renoir did not represent such an obvious detachment, such a marked leaning away from the Impressionist trend. He marked himself off, however, by the prime importance that he gave to the human figure (in the portrait, during the first part of his life; in the nude, during the second). As with Degas, but to a lesser extent, his portraits are not anonymous persons, but well-characterised individuals.

Like Cézanne and Degas, Renoir was less preoccupied than the other painters with catching the moment. If he used vibrant colours and short strokes in his technique, it was only because he was seeking a more sharply defined likeness in spite of his glowing movement.

Claude Monet and his emulators painted the epidermis of the world; one does not feel the sap flowing in their trees. Renoir, on the contrary, makes us feel the blood coursing under the skin of each of his models.

MINOR MASTERS

Impressionism was not only the passionate affirmation of a few great artists brought together by chance. It became a great movement because it could attract painters of little importance who, however, contributed to its spreading; for outside the group proper, and mainly in the provinces, there existed some kindred sensibilities who were like an echo for a public that was often deprived of the possibility of direct contact.

Berthe Morisot   Cherry Picking   Madame Ernest Rouart Collection, Paris

Of these minor masters, a number in Paris very soon sided with the new ideas. Certain of them even figured in some of the exhibitions: Lebourg, Lépine and Guillaumin were among them. Caillebotte did even more: his material circumstances made it possible for him to buy his friends' work and thus he assembled a magnificent collection. However, this caused a scandal when, in 1893, he bequeathed it to the Luxembourg Museum. Of the sixty-seven pictures offered, the State refused twenty-nine. (Three Cézannes, three Degas, two Manets, eight Monets, eleven Pissarros, two Renoirs and three Sisleys.)

Fantin-Latour must be named among the painters who were in favour of Impressionism. His technique could not be linked with this aesthetic standpoint, but he was a friend of the group's, and one is indebted to him for a composition that, under the title *L'atelier aux Batignolles*, gathered Bazille, Monet, Renoir, Zacharie Astruc and Emile Zola around Manet. Zola was, in fact, an ardent and courageous defender of the new ideas; for having written a eulogy of Manet, in 1866, he even had to discontinue his contributions to the journal *l'Evénement*. But this enthusiasm was not to last, for in 1880 Zola was writing: « They are all forerunners. They remain inferior to the work they attempt; they stammer without being able to find their words »... and at the time of the open subscription whose purpose was to get « Olympia » accepted into the national collections, he replied to Monet, who had solicited his help: « ...I am utterly against buying pictures, even for the Louvre. That lovers of painting should club together to raise the prices of a painter whose canvasses they have acquired, I can understand; but I have promised myself, I, a writer, never to get myself mixed up in this sort of affair... ».

In the provinces, Impressionism had no immediate impact. There were few adepts, but one must nevertheless mention some individuals whose aims evinced an obvious kinship. Guigou had already shown an interest in landscape observed on the spot in the Corot-Daubigny manner, but with the structure and, above all, the light so peculiar to Provence.

Claude Monet Hay-ricks
Crayon drawing. Private Collection, Paris

Camille Pissarro The Woodcutter. 1878
Musée du Louvre, Paris

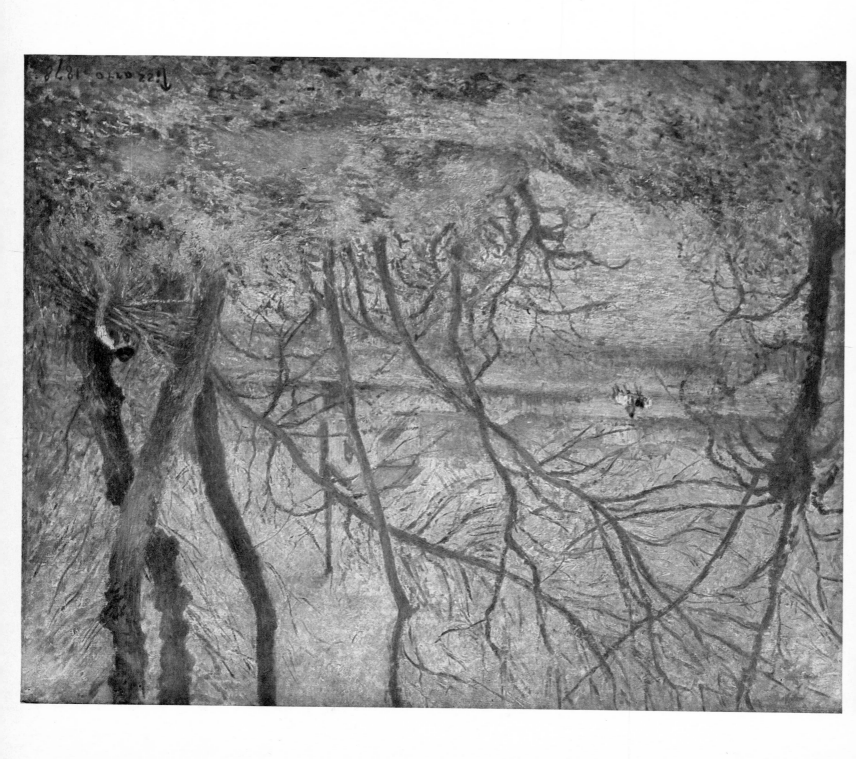

Paul Cézanne A Modern Olympia. 1873
Musée du Louvre, Paris

Paul Cézanne Self-Portrait. 1877
Bayerische Staatsgemälde Collection, Munich

Paul Cézanne Portrait of Madame Cézanne. c. 1883
Black-stone drawing. Boymans Museum, Rotterdam

Paul Cézanne L'Amour de Puget. c. 1888
Crayon drawing. Brooklyn Museum, New York

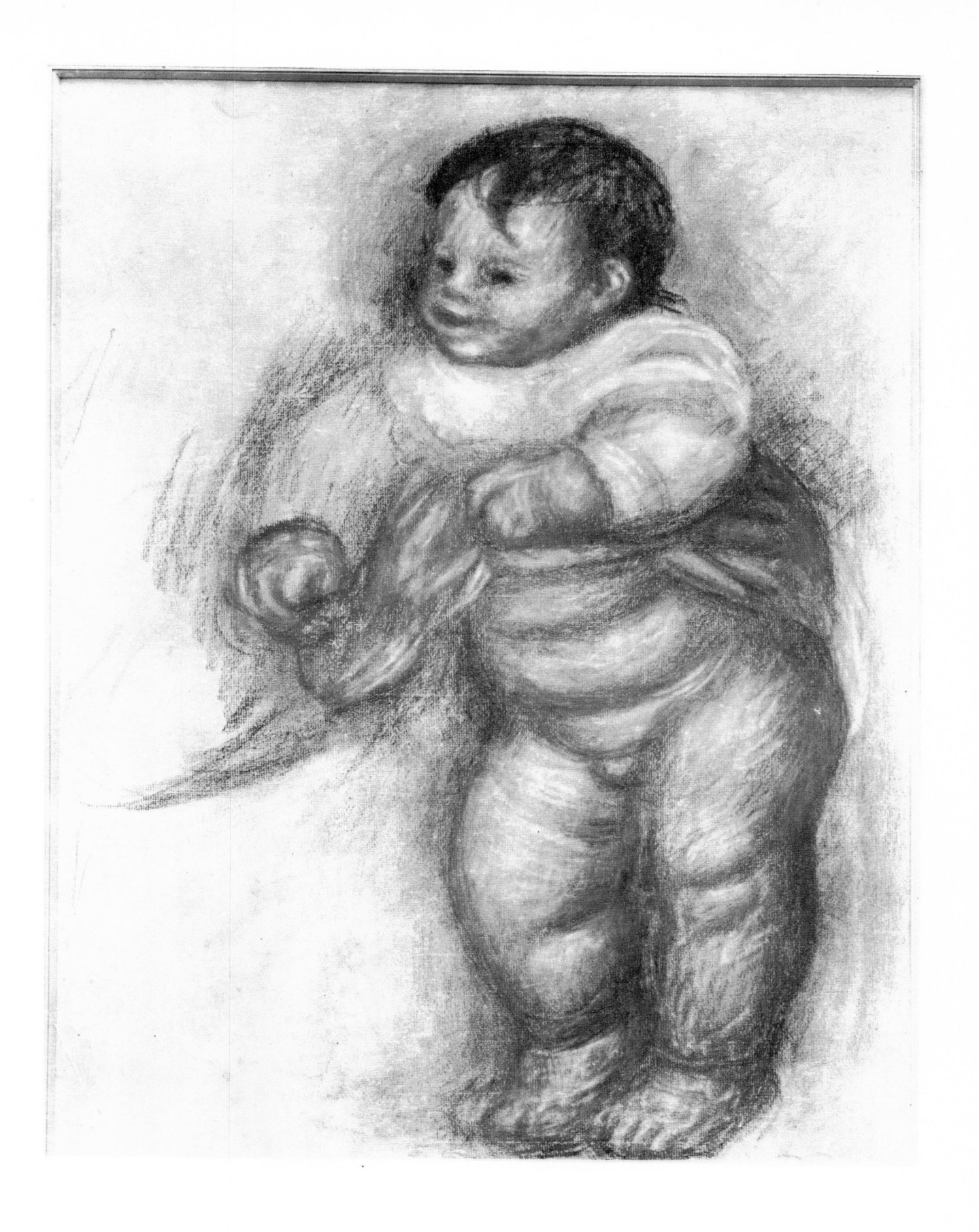

Pierre-Auguste Renoir Study.
Black-lead drawing. Albright Art Gallery, Buffalo, N.Y.

Paul Cézanne Portrait of Achille Empereire. 1877
Charcoal. Musée des Beaux-Arts, Basel

Paul Cézanne Woman with a Coffee-Pot. 1890-94 Musée du Louvre, Paris

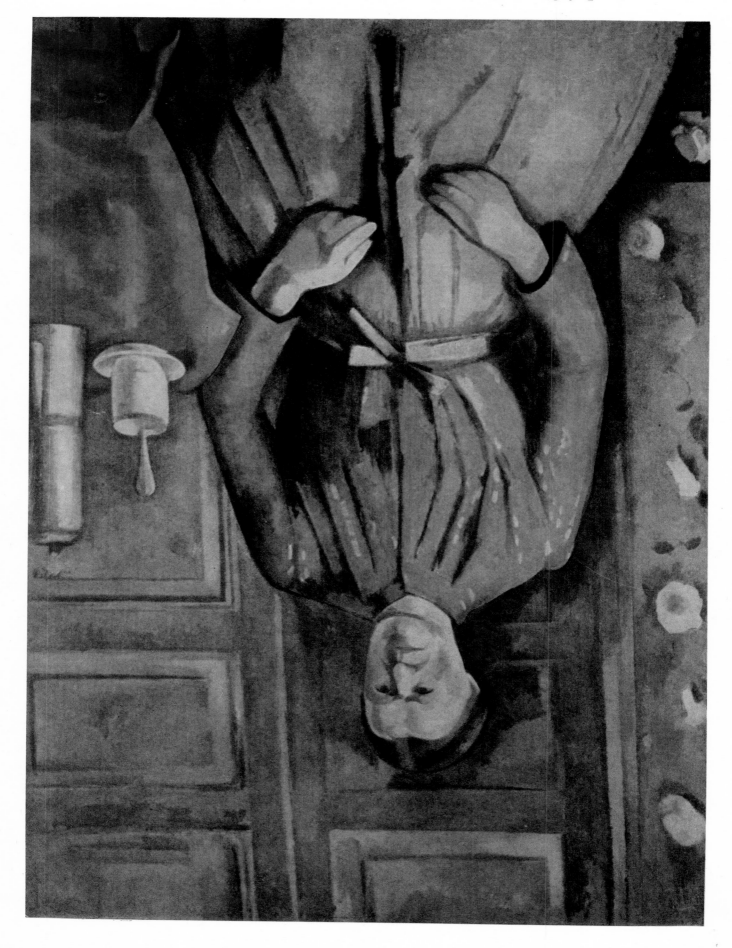

Pierre-Auguste Renoir   Le Moulin de la Galette (Detail). 1876
Musée du Louvre, Paris

Edouard Manet The Barmaid. 1878
Musée du Louvre, Paris

Paul Cézanne Portrait of Victor Choquet. c. 1875
Lord Rothschild Collection, Merton Hall, Cambridge, England

In Marseilles, Monticelli was showing an even closer kinship, through his technique of overlaid strokes, which created a luminous surface. Yet, his choice of themes, his theatrical taste for composed scenes, the small attraction that subjects in their natural state held for him – these prevented him from joining Monet and his friends, although there are glimmerings of the magic of reality in him.

In Lyons, three painters defended the merits of colour: Ravier, a painter of striking still lifes; Vernay, of eerie landscapes and, even more, Carrand, whose almost monochrome canvasses exude a secret poetry that corresponds to what the Intimists revealed some years later.

SECOND GENERATION: AT THE PINNACLE OF REASON

When the *Salon des Artistes Indépendants* was founded in 1884, Impressionism had won the battle. Even if its early apostles still encountered serious difficulties, its supporters and admirers were too numerous from then on for the impetus to be checked; events were already taking shape, some to swell it, others, before long, to work against it. In fact, a new generation embraced Impressionism when it was beginning to be accepted but seemed to have blunted its edge and lost its impact; the work of its pioneers appeared almost too careful in face of the brand-new passion that fired the new drive. Very quickly, but without rebelling against their elders, this rising generation was moving towards extremes: either the extreme of theory and reasoning, or the extreme of passion and inspiration.

At the first *Salon des Indépendants*, Seurat showed « La baignade ». But it was in 1886, at the eighth and last Impressionist exhibition, that the Divisionist technique appeared, focused and proclaimed by Seurat, and illustrated at this *Salon* by his chief work: « la grande Jatte ».

Until then, the Impressionist technique had certainly leaned on theories, but these, in fact, were more or less invented subsequently and did not impose an over-strict discipline on the artists. Rather, each was left to interpret the doctrine intuitively and very freely.

In banding together under the Neo-Impressionist, or Divisionist, banner, Seurat and his friends (notably Signac and Henry-Edmond Cros) were trying to put some order into the revolution and establish some firm principles. Thus, nothing more was to be left to chance: neither the choice of colours, nor the upward or downward movement of line, nor even the size of brushstroke. The revolution brought about by the forerunners led to the formulation of rules as strict as those of the *Académie*, but, however, infinitely more vital and fresh. Seurat laid down the principles of his aesthetics very precisely, and dictated them to his biographer, Jules Christophe:

« Art is harmony; harmony is the analogy of opposites (contrasts), the analogy of like things (degraded), of tone, of line; tone is light and shade; tint is red and its complement, green, or orange and blue, or yellow and violet; line is the slope on a horizontal. These different harmonies are quiet, gay or sad; the gaiety of tone is in its dominant luminosity; of tint, in its dominant warmth; of line, in the rising slopes (beyond the horizontal); the quietness of tone is in the balance of light and shade; of tint, in the balance of warmth and coldness; and of line, in the balance of the horizontals. The sadness of tone is in its dominant sombreness; of tint, in its dominant coldness; and of line in the downward slope. The mode of expression is the optical mixture of tones, and of tints and the shadows they produce, following very fixed laws.

« To divide is:

« To make sure of all the benefits of luminosity, colour, and harmony by:

1. The optical mixture of uniquely pure pigments (all the colours of the prism and their tones)·

2. the separation of various elements (local colour, colour of lighting, their effects, etc.);
3. the balance of these elements and their proportion (according to the laws of contrast, degradation and irradiation);
4. the choice of a brush-stroke proportionate with the dimensions of the picture.

« To paint in dots is:

« The mode of expression chosen by the painter who prefers to put colour on a canvas in little dots, rather than spread it out flat, with no mind for balance, and careless of contrast. The dot is only a brush-stroke, a method, and, like all methods, hardly matters. »

The enthusiastic welcome and faithfulness of some painters – Albert Dubois-Pillet, Maximilien Luce, Hippolyte Petitjean, Lucie Cousturier, Théo van Rysselberghe – were to be insufficient to spread this new doctrine very widely. Nevertheless, it gave birth to some works of high enough quality for the « Neo-Impressionist » school still to fill an irreplaceable chapter in the history of contemporary painting.

AT THE PINNACLE OF INSPIRATION

This prolongation of Impressionism – which was at the same time its limitation – was soon to be followed by a reaction, which was instinctive and had important consequences.

Van Gogh and Gauguin are cases in point. They gave themselves over to painting with a passion approaching mysticism, and served it as if in furious combat, as if sacrificing their lives to a faith.

Pierre-Auguste Renoir Three Bathers. 1882
Black-lead. Musée du Louvre, Paris

Paul Cézanne Trees
Albright Art Gallery, Buffalo, N.Y.

Edgar Degas Dancer Crayon drawing. Paris

Pierre-Auguste Renoir Portrait of Lucie Bérard. 1884
Maurice Bérard Collection, Paris

Edouard Manet   Portrait of Lina Campineanu.   1878   William Rockhill Nelson Gallery of Art, Kansas City

Edgar Degas The Dancing Class. c. 1874
Musée du Louvre, Paris

96

Edgar Degas At the Café-Concert («Les Ambassadeurs»). 1875 Musée du Louvre, Paris

Edgar Degas The Singer with Glove. 1878
Harvard University, Fogg Art Museum, Maurice Wertheim Collection, Cambridge, Massachusetts

Paul Cézanne   The Blue Vase. 1883-87   Musée du Louvre, Paris

Van Gogh did it with the spiritual detachment of a hermit buried in the solitude of his conviction, working feverishly under the impulse of the divine word, but living humbly before the greatness of what he was seeking to accomplish; Gauguin did it with the pride of a conqueror who calls up fresh forces after each new failure, because he sees in the ordeal a proof of the sublime nature of his mission, and feels that he is the incarnation of a genius – even if he dare not utter the word – thanks to which he can live through the worst hours without falling into despair, and, above all, without his work causing him the least trace of discouragement.

Moreover, it is interesting to notice that these two artists – prototypes of the « possessed painter », which modern art has multiplied – who were so tried by fate, let nothing of the moral and material difficulties that assailed them appear in their art.

Their position was in direct contrast with that of the Romanticists. They opened new perspectives on the future.

Van Gogh, in his mystical restlessness, his impetuosity, and in the distortions that he imposed on Nature with his flaming trees, blazing suns, and twisted branches, prepared for the advent of Expressionism which, following on from him, was even to use caricature to express the tension in a torn humanity.

Paul Cézanne   Bathers. c. 1890
Lithograph

Edgar Degas Dancer. 1889
Crayon drawing. The Art Institute of Chicago

Gauguin was to try to recapture Classical order, without shutting out sentiment; he first sought this order, which had nothing to do with the intellectualisations of a Seurat, in an accumulation of signs and symbols. For years he was faithful to Impressionism and, during his first stays in Brittany, had followed Moret, Maufra and Loiseau-painters who were connected with the movement and, although among neither the forerunners nor the initiators, had learnt from their elders, and were producing work of great dignity, without feeling the need, in their turn, to invent new means of expression.

Gauguin was not content with this submission. After having benefited from their experience, he tried to free himself by discussing ideas, and by introducing extra-pictorial features into painting (the very thing that the pure Impressionists were vigorously resisting, since they wanted to make a picture an end in itself, independent of its subject).

Thus, Gauguin found himself mixed up in a reaction that tended to spiritualise art and, under the title of « Synthesism » corresponded to the Symbolist current in literature. But this intellectualisation was too far from painting itself and Gauguin, moreover, felt it was too dependent on writers; his unruly temperament kicked against it. He certainly felt the necessity of a discipline that would help him recapture the purity of a Classical art, but if he was to accept this discipline, it had to stem from him. Now, what the Symbolists proposed to him, ill accorded with the attraction he felt for exotic sumptuousness. In order to find this, he was to go as far as the Antipodes and, among Tahitian landscapes, and in contact with Maori tribes, he was to invent

Georges Seurat Couple Dancing. c. 1886
Crayon and pen-and-ink drawing. Private Collection, Paris

Georges Seurat The Artist in his Studio. c. 1884
The Philadelphia Museum of Art. A. E. Gallatin Collection

104

Georges Seurat Study. c. 1888
Black-stone and black-lead. Private Collection, Paris

Georges Seurat Study of an Old Woman Black-stone J. Rodriguez-Henriques Collection, Paris

106

Edgar Degas Women Combing their Hair. 1875
Water-colour. Phillips Memorial Gallery, Washington, D.C.

a modern Classicism for himself, and a range of perfect forms, barbaric and refined, at once inspired and reasoned, that was one of the most powerful creations of the Anti-Impressionist reaction. At any rate, be it with Van Gogh – that is to say, with an art dominated by instinct – or with Gauguin – that is to say, with an art dominated by will – we find ourselves before a breaking-up of Impressionism; wishing to go beyond what it had achieved, these two artists adopted an attitude that was a kind of denial. They believed they were remaining faithful to Impressionism even while seeking a more complete concept in painting pure and simple; but is it really keeping within the limits of painting pure and simple to load a picture with ideas as complex as theirs? One must not lose sight of the fact that, with them, the introduction of religious sentiment, so alien to the Impressionists, was a means of turning Art away from its true ends.

Unquestionably, Cézanne, Monet or Degas unfailingly illustrate the principles of « Art for Art's sake »; but because of the fact that he devoted just as much of his energy to getting his worries out of his system, Van Gogh no longer used painting for itself but as a means to an end; he gave himself away as much in his pictures as in his letters, and some of these ideas are not so very far from what Seurat said about the significance of colours.

A picture by Van Gogh is so richly charged with meaning, that it permits of as many interpretations as a poem of that period. Spontaneous as it was, this art, with all its overtones, was very close to literature.

In other ways, Gauguin tended towards a more or less analogous attitude – although it seems so different – since he also gave symbolic value to a figure. This analogy explains the two men's

Puvis de Chavannes La Toilette. 1883
Charcoal drawing. Private Collection, Paris

Pierre-Auguste Renoir Baigneuse. 1880 ▷
Musée Rodin, Paris

Jean-Baptiste-Armand Guillaumin Landscape. 1898
Private Collection, Paris

Paul Cézanne Peasant in Blue Smock. 1895
Mrs. T. G. Kenefick Collection, Buffalo, New York

Paul Cézanne Portrait of a Man (The Watchmaker). 1895 Solomon Guggenheim Museum, New York

friendship and the error they made in believing that together they could accomplish their destiny and their life's work. The stay in Arles was the crowning moment of their journey together; it also underlines, in the cruelest way, the differences that made the break inevitable, even if there was no drama in it. They both believed in obeying their instincts and, at the same time, in discussing their work. Doubtless, they were sincere; the numerous writings they left indisputably testify to that. With Van Gogh, reasoning came after creation, as if to justify his inspired methods. But with Gauguin, reasoning came first; then intuition stepped in to remove whatever might have been dessicated, and made a formula into a living language, capable of adapting itself to changes. Thus, Van Gogh could not become the leader of a school of painting; using him as a criterion, one would not have known how to work out a system that he himself had not conceived; but he was to serve as an example to future generations, not because it was necessary to imitate him either in his life or his work, but simply because of the inspiring lessons to be learnt from them. But from Gauguin, it was easy to plan out an entire set of logical ideas, constituting a return to the purest Classicism, a set of ideas in which Man dominates his work. We are far from caring about reality, about life in its separate moments: but these were basic to the Impressionist theories; we find ourselves here before artists who felt they had a mission to accomplish and for whom painting was not only a mystical act but a vital function.

It is permissible to believe that here lay their most important role. The Impressionists achieved a break with Art as it had existed since the Renaissance; Gauguin and Van Gogh profited from this break to build a new world. Impressionism was not constructive and was only of value to itself, whilst Van Gogh and Gauguin established the foundations of an order in which the artist is no longer a simple artisan, but the inspired messenger, the one who hurries along the secret ways that humanity seek. Towards the end of the century, Cézanne was to start exercising a considerable influence because, in him too, aesthetics can be constituted from the point of view of the painting; but this is exclusively pictorial and involves no philosophical position for Man, while with Van Gogh and Gauguin, the work of art is a reflection, a consequence, of Man's life. With both painters, Art definitely stepped out of its figurative role. The picture had become an allusion to reality and, if one takes the trouble to analyse the composition of some of Gauguin's paintings, one is forced to admit that red bananas, yellow trees and violet meadows are not true images, not even transpositions, but a complete invention, which becomes true because it establishes a human equilibrium through the fine balance of colours and forms. In Van Gogh, the individual vocabulary had supplanted the principles of the School; Gauguin understood the risk of disorder in this liberty, and tried to achieve discipline without stifling the individual imagination. Thus, these two forms of art, which were at the limits of madness and misery, and were like a shining full stop to Impressionism, were to serve as a more or less acknowledged starting-point for the freest ideologies that the painters of the 20th century were to embrace.

THE THIRD GENERATION

The mystical-symbolic movement that Gauguin had touched upon, corresponded to another movement and did not cease when Gauguin went his own way. It brought together some artists whom we shall call « the third generation ». After the excesses of reason or violence of the second generation, they wanted to find a quieter life. The example of the tumultuous lives of Van Gogh or Gauguin drove them to a meditative withdrawal; but that given by Renoir, Cézanne, Monet or Degas appealed more to their character.

Vincent Van Gogh   The Harvest in Provence. 1888
Water-colour and pen-and-ink drawing. Private Collection, Wistinghausen

Of course, they were interested in the experiments of Seurat and Gauguin, and when Sérusier, after having spent several months with Gauguin in Brittany during the year 1888, brought back the picture called « The Talisman », painted in accordance with the ideas of the new prophet, he won an enthusiastic following from his friends of the Julian Academy. However, in the association that these men formed at that time under the name of « Nabis », emotion probably played a more decisive part than artistic truth; one was the result of the other and they amused themselves creating their own esoteric world.

Is it the desire to escape banality, or the urge to serve God, that one should look for in these painters, in their pseudo-religiosity? Their position was probably more intellectual than truly Christian, and the taste for secret sects counted for at least as much as real faith. The artist aspired to a further advance, in both his way of life and his work, so as to add to the *reportage* of the Impressionists a silence that would be like the reflection of an inner life, so as to give the appearance of things a more deeply human undertone, one that would reveal more of the soul. Odilon Redon, who belonged to the first generation of Impressionists, had already started giving form to mystery and creating a world where phantoms took the place of real beings; even when he painted flowers, he gave them a dull, supernatural lustre, and the strange look of dying stars, about to fade but still gleaming bright, gathering their last strength.

114

The symbolism at which Gauguin aimed was more elementary and superficial, and was part of a series of experiments in which, on the pretext of finding a new symbology, the artists were searching primarily for a synthesis of forms; in fact, they took more interest in the discovery of novel aesthetics than in the possibility of bringing a mystical message into their art.

Emile Bernard, particularly, played an important part in this process, both as far as the doctrine and the pictorial technique were concerned. He had been attached to the Nabis group in which this movement was given definite shape – a movement of which Maurice Denis was to become the apostle; and Denis, who was more exclusively attached to Christianity, was to be the mainspring of the great effort for the restoration of religious painting that was to develop in the following years. Bonnard and Vuillard were to renounce the secret societies dear to their youth, but were always to keep that intimate sense of humanity that opened up depths to Impressionism – depths that were richer than those afforded by the observation of Nature and nothing else. Just as the Impressionists found their ideal theme in landscape, in the dazzle of brilliant sunshine where their joyful discovery of luminous painting came to flower, so did Bonnard, Vuillard and also – but to a lesser extent – Maurice Denis find their ideal subject in the study of interior scenes. The softened tonalities, even the harmonies of greys, were as expressive, as varied to them as the most sonorous modulations of their elders.

It may be that, through the very excess of their genius, the Impressionists gave these newcomers the idea that the resources of the open air were exhausted, and that it was time to explore places less frequented by painters.

Vincent Van Gogh Boats at Saintes Maries. 1888
Pen and reed. Tschudi Collection, Munich

Vincent Van Gogh Landscape, 1890
Black-lead. V. W. Van Gogh Collection, Amsterdam

In fact, when Bonnard and Vuillard approached the open air, they did it in a completely differ-ent attitude of mind from that of their elders. One does not feel a sensation of space, of a distant horizon, in their pictures, as one does in Monet. One senses more the quiet stillness, the narrow limits of interior scenes. The matching half-tints are a sign of intimacy; in the freshest colours, the tempting call of grisailles can be felt; these painters always seem to prefer shady corners to the violence of brilliant sunshine.

Even in K.X. Roussel, who devoted himself exclusively to landscape, we are conscious of a similar feeling of intimacy, even when he contrives mythological scenes with fauns and nymphs. His Parnassus belongs to a quiet, tasteful bourgeoisie; he is without either triviality or excessive gran-deur; his Gods are made to people well-kept parks on wealthy estates in the neighborhood of Paris. Such discretion, such prudence, did not exclude talent, however; if they had not been generously gifted with it, these artists would have probably only achieved minor art. But, behind the modest façade, men who were real painters were trying to renew contact with everyday life, with the art that grows out of society, the art that, in the most varied forms, had triumphed for centuries. They were not tempted by the revolts and scandals that had succeeded one another since Romanticism; to avoid making a still more assertive challenge, they satisfied themselves with a

116

Paul Gauguin Tahitian Woman's Head. 1896
Crayon drawing. Private Collection, New York

Henri de Toulouse-Lautrec   Negro Dancer in the Achille Bar. 1896
Musée de Toulouse-Lautrec, Albi

118

Lithograph
Odilon Redon The Marsh Flower. 1885

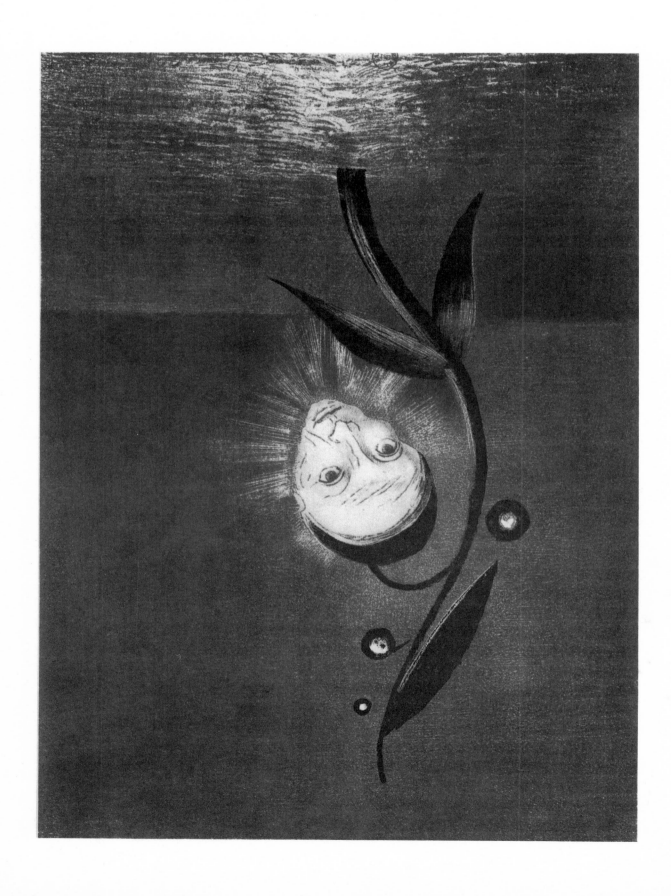

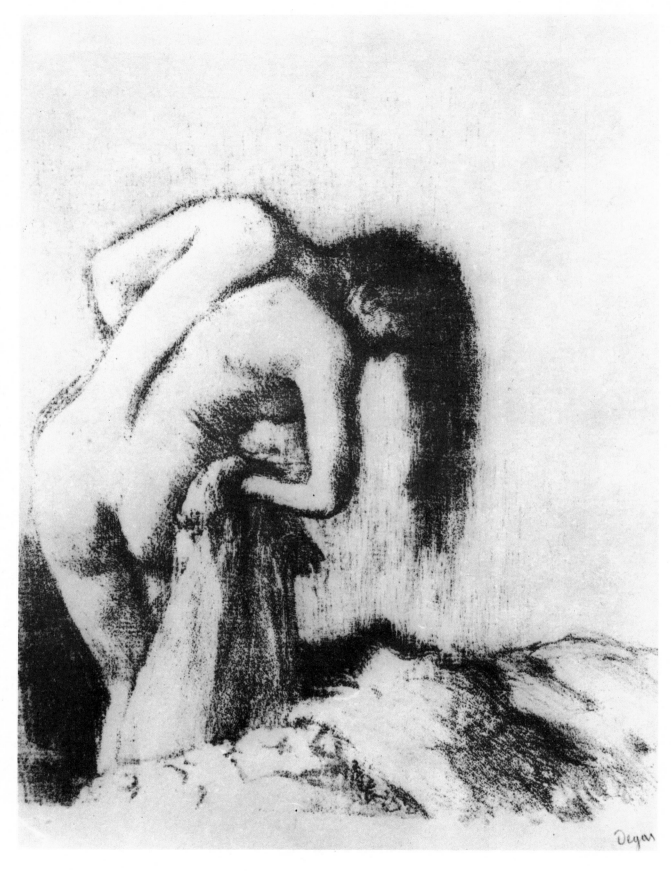

Edgar Degas After the Bath. 1890
Lithograph.

Pierre-Auguste Renoir Small Blue Nude. 1882
Albright Art Gallery, Buffalo, N.Y. ▷

120

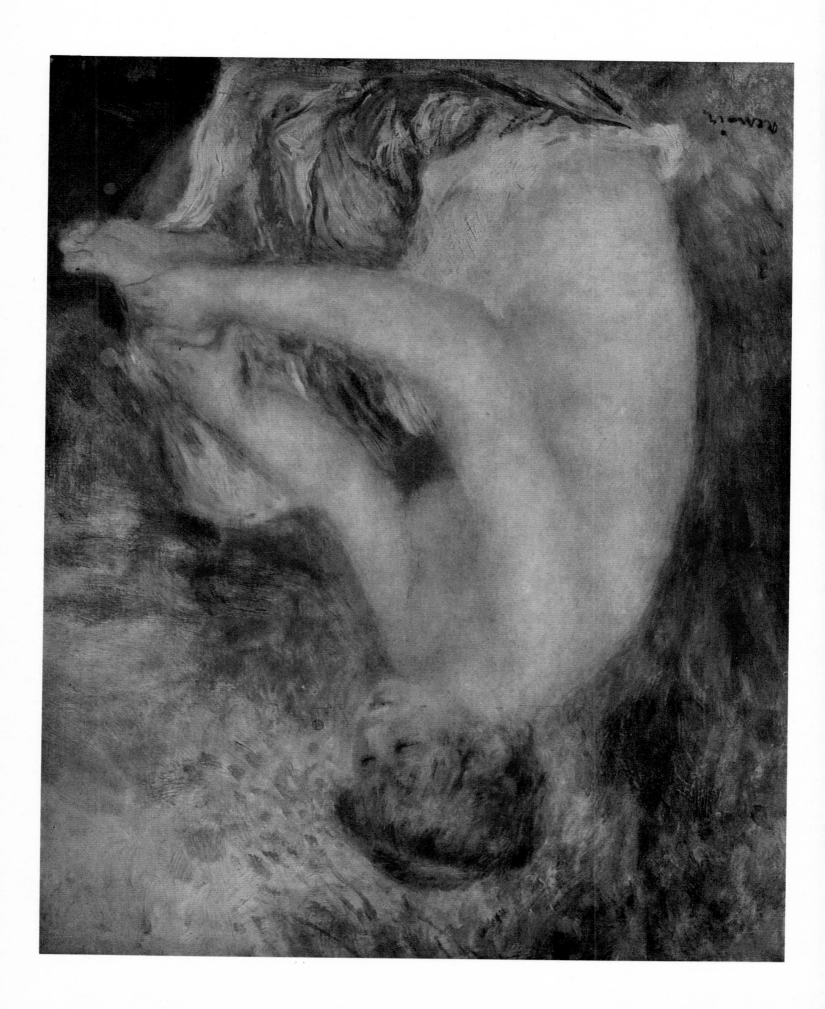

Edouard Manet Vase of Flowers. 1880 Féral Collection, Paris

122

Pierre-Auguste Renoir Roses of Vargemont. 1882
Private Collection, Paris

Georges Seurat
The Seine at
Courbevoie. 1885
Ittleson Collection
New York

Georges Seurat
Woman with Parasol
Study for
«La Grande Jatte». 1884
Emil G. Buehrle Collection
Zurich

125

Georges Seurat Profile of Woman Posing. 1888 Musée du Louvre, Paris

Georges Seurat The Circus. 1890-91 Musée du Louvre, Paris

Vincent van Gogh Head of a Peasant. Nuenen, 1885
Dr. G. Schweitzer Collection, Berlin

Vincent van Gogh   Old Peasant of Provence. 1888
Chester Beatty Collection, London

Vincent van Gogh The Pear-Tree in Blossom. Arles, 1888
V. W. Van Gogh Collection, Amsterdam

130

Vincent van Gogh   The Town Hall of Auvers on July 14th. 1890
Mr. and Mrs. Leigh B. Block's Collection, Chicago

131

Paul Gauguin Breton Girls. 1889
Private Collection, Paris

Paul Gauguin « Les Alyscamps ». 1888
Musée du Louvre, Paris

Paul Gauguin
Girl with Mango. 1892
Museum of Art
Cone Collection, Baltimore

Paul Gauguin Woman with Fruit (Detail). Tahiti, 1893
Hermitage, Leningrad

Paul Gauguin Still Life. 1901
Emil G. Buehrle Collection, Zurich

Henri de Toulouse-Lautrec   The Divan. 1893
Sao Paulo Museum, Brasil

138

Henri de Toulouse-Lautrec Resting. 1896 Private Collection, Brussels

Henri de Toulouse-Lautrec Woman Dressing. 1896
Musée du Louvre, Paris

Henri de Toulouse-Lautrec Portrait of Mr. Fourcade. 1889
Sao Paulo Museum, Brasil

141

Paul Cézanne   Jourdan's Hut (Last picture painted by Cézanne). 1906
Kunstmuseum, Basel

142

Odilon Redon The Sphinx, c. 1900
Rijksmuseum Kroeller-Mueller, Otterloo

Claude Monet The Parliament in London. 1904
Musée du Louvre, Paris

Paul Signac St. Tropez, 1906
French Art Galleries, New York

Pierre Bonnard View of Cannet. 1935 Private Collection, Paris

Edouard Vuillard Interior. 1910 Private Collection, Paris

more secret message, murmured in an undertone, like a dialogue between initiates.

Their movement did not seek to convince the public at large; it had the honesty of lives that rolled on without forethought or sudden fits. This being the case, these artists gave Man a place again, since it is Man, whether he is present or not, who gives each of their pictures its atmosphere. The garden becomes the extension of the drawing-room.

While the Nabis stayed at home or affectionately kept an eye on their friends' apartments, another painter, Toulouse-Lautrec – drawn into the Impressionist movement by Degas rather than by Monet – sought a solution and new inspiration in the artificial world of public dances and the theatre. He brought the same fresh observation to this artificial life, with its powdered women and stage-lighting and décor, that Monet had put into the evocation of the countryside of Ile-de-France. He loved the acid colours with which he created unexpected harmonies, with which he extolled the most ordinary subjects. The elegance and sureness of his incisive drawing, the freshness of his palette, never deserted him and, before the most trivial subject, he always maintained the detached purity of Oriental artists, by whom his art had been influenced.

Morally speaking, Toulouse-Lautec was the antithesis of the Nabis; he affected to reject society; each of his portraits constitutes a severe judgement on his contemporaries; but his way of life was not a conscious reaction against Impressionism. If there is almost no landscape in his work, especially after he had asserted his own personality, and if he devoted himself exclusively to the human being, to attitudes and faces, this choice was not for him a way of opposing the work of his predecessors, or of adding to it. One must rather see it as a form of revenge: deprived by his infirmity of the physical fulfilment he had hoped for, kept by circumstances on the fringe of his social milieu, he rushed, like a desperate man, to the opposite extreme. He despised women because he could not conquer them; he ignored the countryside because he felt out of place in it. He looked at the disinherited and the corrupted with a restless attention, at once cruel and compassionate, and this resentment was his way of bringing Man back into the art of his time, his way of exalting Man's weaknesses. He gave reality and a lasting quality to the artificial. Through the place that he restored to the human being, Toulouse-Lautrec obtained a result analogous to that achieved by the Nabis, although he arrived at it by other methods. Thus, moderation and revolt joined hands, as if episodes counted for little in the final reckoning.

Besides their qualities as painters, all these artists played the role of witnesses in their time, and today we realise better that their contemporaries did not. They were the last to leave us a precise image of a society that was soon to disappear and that the Impressionists were not generally at pains to represent, with the partial exception of Renoir in certain pictures (painted around 1867-1880) and Degas in some of his portraits. Let us stress that, in these last two painters, this representation concerned well-defined characters, as much as it did in Bonnard, Vuillard and Toulouse-Lautrec; but viewed as a whole, the effigies produced by all these painters convey an over-all sense of the period, as though the characters were anonymous, and it is doubtless this factor that forged the closest link between the two generations. It is even more significant that these newcomers started along the path when their elders had renounced it.

Impressionism had virtually reached the end of its evolution. Van Gogh had been its last spark; the Nabis, the last warm glow of its dying embers. Impressionism saw its destiny draw to a close with the century that had seen its birth and growth. All that was to follow was to be a mere succession of rejections or denials.

◁ *Pierre Bonnard* Still Life. Last picture painted by Bonnard. 1946
Gallery Maeght, Paris

Paul Signac Ships. 1932
Water-colour. Private Collection, Paris

ACADEMICISM

Against all expectations, Impressionism fairly soon mustered supporters in the circles that seemed least likely to welcome it and, if it is paradoxical that Renoir's first successes stemmed from the right-thinking Parisian bourgeoisie, it is still more astonishing to find the new ideas adapted by artists who, at the same time, were currying official favour and later became part of the *Institut*. The *Salon des Artistes Francais* was obstinate in refusing the work sent in by Manet, Renoir and Cézanne; but it was soon contaminated in spite of itself, and quickly saw its most brilliant members bow to the influence it abhorred. Several young painters, fresh from *l'Ecole*, loaded with *Prix de Rome* and other awards, applied their skilful technique to luminous colour and transformed the popular Impressionist revolt into a pseudo-boldness, acceptable to society people.

Carolus Duran was a Manet who knew how to please. Gervex did for young women of society what Renoir had done for working girls. Albert Besnard transformed the fiery suns of Turner and Manet into harmless fireworks; it was in connection with this that Degas made his famous quip: « They are firemen who catch fire ».

When Divisionism appeared and lent new energy to the revolt, Seurat quickly found some emulators where he was not expecting them. Henri Martin started painting in short regular strokes, and went on to paint numerous pictures, which decorated the Capitol of Toulouse.

Ernest Laurent and Aman-Jean stood by the ideas of their friend Seurat, but did not go as far as applying his system rigorously. Le Sudaner, who came a little later, was also to adopt the

Lithograph
Pierre Bonnard   Woman Bathing, 1934

technique of division by short strokes, but he did so in order to achieve soft harmonies and a velvety atmosphere-which in the eyes of his public, made up for the originality of his technique. Manet, on the other hand, was to have a direct influence on Jacques-Emile Blanche, a painter gifted with unquestionable qualities as an observer and critic. He was to build up a portrait of the society of his time, and his art, which was not without a certain snobbish tone, remains one of the most lively images of worldly society at the end of the 19th century and the beginning of the 20th.

In the same vein, and with the same short, flowing brush-strokes and keen observation, Forain was also a witness; but he recorded ideas rather than people. In spite of all his wit, and because his criticisms lacked a generous soul behind them, he never achieved the human qualities that there are in Daumier' work.

Even very dedicated men like Henner or Hébert could not be called complete strangers to Impressionism, or said to have ignored the current of ideas that produced it. Their reactions to it were a kind of recognition and Hébert, best known as a portraitist, painted some landscapes that prove he was interested in them as a subject, although he tried to hide it. For his part, Bonnat sometimes took certain liberties with his brush-stroke, and in this way gave Manet's liberties official sanction, although he was not as independent in his choice of colour.

More authentic, more essential, was the contribution made by three painters whom it would not be right to call opponents of the new painting and whose work was complementary to it. Carrière was a sort of Impressionist of the sentiments, making faces emerge from the mist as Monet had

Henri-Edmond Cross Landscape. 1910
Water-colour. Private Collection, Paris

Maurice Denis Nude Study, 1930
Crayon drawing, Private Collection, Paris

done with cathedrals, and finding in this a chance to insist on the character of his model even more than the form.

Puvis de Chavannes was often to take his place with the rebels because he, too, was looking for an art that was not mere imitation, an art that would find the grandeur of a style in life. He was to meet Gauguin – who was not sparing in his admiration for him – in various circumstances. Finally, Gustave Moreau achieved more than the invention of a fantastic world, similar to Redon's but much more dazzling. He was also the teacher at the *Ecole des Beaux-Arts* whose lessons proved such a magnificent help to Matisse, Marquet, Jean Puy, Rouault and others, thus preparing for Fauvism, the sequel to Impressionism which was to emerge at the beginning of the 20th century.

Winslow Homer The Apple Bee. 1890
Wood engraving. The Art Institute of Chicago

SUPPORTERS AND OPPONENTS ABROAD

The importance of Impressionism in the 19th century, and the light it spread, lay not only in the exceptional quality of the artists who made it glorious, but also in the fact that in it they were giving solid form to ideas that were still not completely formulated and were awaiting the opportunity to be crystallized. Two of the most important of these ideas, let us remember, were on the one hand the artist's desire to express himself freely, to substitute his own truth, in a work of art, for that of the outside world and, on the other hand, his need to regain contact with Nature, both

James McNeil Whistler Lithograph

James McNeil Whistler Symphony in White. 1864
Tate Gallery, London ▷

Winslow Homer Croquet Scene. 1864 The Art Institute of Chicago

Albert Pinkham Ryder Cove in the Moonlight. c. 1890
Phillips Memorial Gallery, Washington D.C.

Louis-Michel Eilshemius On the Shore. c. 1918
Private Collection, New York

161

Telemaco Signorini View of Settignano. The « Piazzetta »
Stramezzi Collection, Milan

162

Max Slevogt Landscape. 1905
Musée des Beaux-Arts, Bern

Gustav Klimt The Church of St. Wolfgang. 1916
Fritz Boeck Collection, Graz

Max Slevogt   Lithograph. Mozart « Don Giovanni »

spiritually and materially, and to make it his inspiration and theme. These two urges took different forms in different countries. Even in those where Impressionism was not to have a profound effect, there was a swing towards the movements that we have mentioned.

Thus, we have seen England, at the beginning of the century, revealing landscape-painters who were forerunners of Impressionism. However, in spite of this start, English art veered away along its own path, and those who had been initiators in French eyes, did not have such a decisive influence in their own country.

On the contrary, the movement that developed after them was marked, above all, by a rejection of new forms; in place of the technical liberties proposed by Constable or Turner, it adopted a smooth, highly-polished style, deliberately impersonal.

Pre-Raphaelitism sought to recover the Renaissance tradition and start out again with the pureness of vision of Rapahel's time; the aim was to serve Romantic-Realist sentimentalism, which is one of the forms of attachment to Nature that we have mentioned.

A number of artists gathered round the initiator, Dante-Gabriel Rossetti; chief among them were John Everet Millais and William Holman Hunt, who were later joined by Ford Madox Brown, and then Burne-Jones. Most important of them all was William Morris, who was to play a considerable part in going beyond the early theories, and was to be one of the most notable creators of the Modern Style and its mannerisms at the end of the century.

The art of the Pre-Raphaelites, lumbered up with innumerable significances and symbols, was in direct opposition to the Impressionists' simple approach to Nature. The most lively reaction against this excessively literary painting came from Whistler, a painter of American origin who, before settling in England, had lived in France for several years, in contact with the Impressionists. In spite of the battles that he fought, and although he was helped by quite a number of support-

165

Arnold Böcklin Landscape Etching

ers, he was unable to make Impressionism a real force in England.

The artist who best helped the expansion of the new ideas, who accepted them and then left the mark of his personality on them, was Walter Sickert. The foundation in 1886 of the New English Art Club, in which he played a part, marked the beginning of a wider understanding; but it was from the beginning of the 20th century onwards that England showed herself more amenable to the currents of thought coming from the Continent, without giving them her unqualified support.

The situation was not the same in the United States, where Impressionism very soon enjoyed great success, thanks to the influence of two artists who had lived in Paris for many years, taking an active part in the movement, and then made it known in their own country. They were Whistler and Mary Cassatt.

Doubtless, Academicism was less fiercely defended in the United States than in Europe; but the majority of the artists there were not ready to throw themselves into a revolutionary adventure and, without altogether lacking personality, they willingly subscribed to accepted ideas. Thomas Eakins had been a pupil of Bonnat and Gérôme in Paris, and some of his pictures evoke something of the early Degas. He remained under the influence of Realism, and belongs more to the Courbet line than to the Impressionist springtime.

One could not say as much for Winslow Homer, who painted the fisherman's harsh life on rough seas, in heavy impastos.

In American painting of this century, Ryder counts for something because of the particular poetic quality that was his reaction against Realism. Later, there was also the naïf charm of Eilshemius, which Marcel Duchamp discovered. There are other artists who prove that Impressionism did not submerge all American art, but in all of them one finds a similar urge to make contact with Nature. Rather paradoxically, Whistler and Mary Cassatt were much less attached to landscape and are better known for their portraits. However, they immediately turned to Impressionism. During his stay in Paris, Whistler took courses at Gleyre's studio, along with Monet, Renoir, Sisley and Bazille; he was a friend of the future Impressionists and exhibited with them at the *Salon des Refusés* of 1863. Then, in 1870, he settled in London where, without renouncing his French friends, he became interested in the Pre-Raphaelites. Mary Cassatt was even more closely connected with the creation, and then the march, of the new artistic movement; a pupil of Renoir and, above all, of Degas – for whom she always had a great admiration – she in fact became the ambassador of Impressionism in America, and was responsible for introducing the great collectors of her country to the canvasses of her former teachers. She herself, a painter of the tenderness of motherhood added a sentimental note to Impressionism which, in her work, completes the familiar landscapes and bold intimacies.

This concern to take daily life, and not Nature properly so-called, as their theme – this was what marked the parallel movements in Holland and Belgium.

While the French concentrated almost exclusively on landscape and hardly bothered to distinguish one place from another, the Belgian and Dutch painters were, on the contrary, influenced by chosen subjects, by the bustle and atmosphere of the towns that inspired them. The work of several of them gives us a composite picture of town life, which went contrary to the French landscape-painters, not only because of its subject but because it revealed, above all, a different way of looking at things.

Max Liebermann Landscape Etching

Apart from Renoir and Degas, the French painters paid little attention to the human being as an individual, and were not concerned to bring out his particular characteristics. But Dutchmen like Breitner and Isaac Israëls were interested in their characters' feelings and their way of life. They observed and painted a town with the same sustained, sensitive care that they would have given to a portrait. If they could not, by virtue of their date of birth, belong to the generation of the first Impressionists, they were among the successors; and to what they received from abroad they added a personal note which established their intermediate position between the German spirit and the French – spirits whose differences are emphasized by contemporary art. While considering the interchange of ideas between France and Holland at the end of the 19th century and the beginning of the 20th, one must not forget to give the Low Countries credit for such an outstanding painter as Van Gogh. He had a close kinship with the artists we have mentioned, notably in his early work. In French Impressionism (from which it would also be incorrect to separate him) he found a liberation in which his genius could flower; yet he did not deny his origins, did not fail to introduce something of his fellow-citizens' view of life into the French tradition.

Another Dutchman, Van Dongen, came a little later, and also added his undeniable gifts to the *Ecole de Paris* and especially to Fauvism; but that belongs to another period, in the first years of the 20th century, when Impressionism was only an indirect and declining influence.

The movement in Belgium was more complex, more varied. Before arriving at Flemish Expressionism, which was a supreme moment in 20th century Belgian painting, her artists followed French painting very closely, either to encourage and spread the movement or to oppose it. As

Edward Munch Seascape Etching

Edward Munch   The Sick Child. 1906
Tate Gallery, London

Max Liebermann At the Canning Factory. 1880
Städtisches Museum, Leipzig

170

Lovis Corinth The Walchensee. 1924
Bayerische Staatsgemälde Collection, Munich

Ferdinand Hodler   Women Running. 1895   Musée des Beaux-Arts, Geneva

Philip Wilson Steer   Girls Running. 1894   Walberswick Pier. Tate Gallery, London

John Sloan Fifth Avenue
Dry-point etching. George F. Porter Collection. The Art Institute of Chicago

in France, academic opposition to the new school of painting was stormily passionate; the battles multiplied and there were warring factions even within groups.

However, a whole Belgian artistic movement was instinctively open to Impressionism, to its taste for painting for its own sake, to the exaltation that lies in the *métier* itself, and to the discovery of light in landscape. Some artists even took a direct part in the French exhibitions. Théo Van Rysselbergh followed the Neo-Divisionist trail blazed by Seurat, and Evenepoel was entirely in the Manet tradition. Rik Wouters, a fine colourist who painted in luminous harmonies, and was often close to Cézanne, had more exuberance but perhaps inferior powers of concentration. Other movements were fighting at the same time to defend regional autonomy. The Laethem-Saint-Martin movement was the best organized and most conscious reaction against French influence – although its commonest theme was also landscape. Artists who illustrate this movement are Georges Minne, de Saedeleer and Van de Woestyne. Their technique was itself a kind of protest against Impressionism: instead of colour laid on in short strokes, they adopted a meticulous precision similar to that of the primitive painters.

Over and above these different movements, there was an artist who played a considerable role and enriched Belgian art of this time with his exceptional personality. He was James Ensor.

Without rejecting Impressionism – he even acknowledged a certain kinship with it – he was far removed from it in the attitudes and symbols that make up his art. The pathetic and aggressive intensity of the subjects that he painted, made him, in company whith the Norwegian Munch, the source of the ideological current that was to give birth to Expressionism. He began by

173

Mary Cassatt The Sisters
Crayon drawing. Museum of Fine Arts, Boston

painting quiet intimate scenes, women in bourgeois settings, and dim lights charged with mystery. Suddenly, he renounced the melancholy charm of the shadows to use colours that were luminous to the point of being acid, so that contrasts were reduced to a minimum; the truculence of his colours links him to the old Flemings; and the burlesque, the macabre caricature, became a violent satire on his time. Puppets people his pictures, with skeletons grimacing behind masks; the most familiar things take on a malefic appearance; each joins in an infernal, grinding saraband. Ensor appeared to take Impressionism as his starting-point; in fact, he had created a tense, disturbing art, diametrically opposed to it.

The other determining influence of Expressionism was, as we have said, that of the Norwegian,

Théo Van Rysselberghe Woman Combing her Hair Black-lead. Private Collection, Brussels

Ferdinand Hodler The Battle of Marignan. 1899
Musée des Beaux-Arts, Bern

Edouard Munch. He was also familiar with Impressionism, and saw a kind of liberation in it; and following a progression similar to that of certain French painters, he threw off this influence while thinking to perpetuate it. Like the Symbolists grouped round Gauguin, Paul Bernard, Sérusier and others, he adopted a more explicit style of painting; he rejected the technique of colour laid on in short strokes and took further liberties of distortion and synthesis. He very soon introduced the idea of the expressive subject; he was moved to pity by suffering humanity, he painted the unrest, nay, even the anguish, of human disappointments and loneliness, and created an art alive with drama, which echoed Ibsen's work in the theatre.

Thus, through him Impressionism tended, in its expansion, towards its own negation and, outside France, led artists along the very road that its founders had eschewed – that of an intellectualism for which painting is a means. For the French, painting had to be an end in itself.

Most of the Scandinavian artists were to follow this new pattern. The Danish painter, Willumsen, for example, who was a friend and follower of Gauguin's, reveals Munch's considerable influence even in his landscapes.

Germany was also to be deeply attracted by Munch's example. It is true that a Realist movement, notably represented by Menzel and Leibl, had previously turned to the art of Courbet; and it owed nothing to the minor Romantic masters from beyond the Rhine.

But Max Liebermann was still more representative of the new style of painting in Germany, because of a conception of landscape and technique whose debt to Impressionism is unmistakable, although Liebermann's art often reveals the attraction that he felt for his subject.

176

BIOGRAPHICAL NOTES

AMAN-JEAN, EDMOND-FRANÇOIS

Born at Chevry-Cossigny (Seine-et-Marne) in 1860. Died in 1935. A painter, engraver and lithographer, his portraits had very personal qualities. His colours especially, with rather quiet shades, suited his drawing well. A close friend of Ernest Laurent and Henri Martin, with whom he shared a travelling scholarship, he accompanied them to Rome in 1885 and adopted the divided technique advocated by his friend Seurat, but without exploiting the effects of colour contrasts. In 1924 he took part with Albert Besnard in the foundation of the Salon des Tuileries.

BAZILLE, FRÉDÉRIC-JEAN

Born at Montpellier 6th December 1841. Died at Beaune-la-Rolande 28th November 1870. Bazille belonged to the Protestant bourgeoisie. Having begun his medical studies at Montpellier, he went to Paris in 1862 to continue them, but was more assiduous in his artistic studies at Gleyre's studio, in company with Claude Monet, Renoir and Sisley, who became his friends. He very soon felt the need to escape study and sought in the open air after themes that suited his taste for fresh colours. Many were the occasions when he painted with Monet near Fontainebleau or Honfleur. In summer he returned to the Mediterranean landscapes. Of all those who were later to be responsible for Impressionism, it was he whose personality was to make itself felt the soonest; his gifts, however, were not to come to full flower for, fighting with the Zouaves during the 1870 War, he was killed at the battle of Beaune-la-Rolande.

BESNARD, ALBERT-PAUL

Born in Paris 2nd June 1849. Died 4th December 1934. Studied first with his father, who was an ex-pupil of Ingres, then at the École des Beaux-Arts in Cabanel's studio. Influenced by the English colourists, he threw himself into the search for colour and the study of composition in order to paint vast mural decorations – at the École de Pharmacie, in the Town Halls of the first and fourth districts, etc. He was also a remarkable portraitist; his portrait of Réjane, particularly, counts among his best work. In 1924 he took part in the foundation of the Salon des Tuileries, of which he was the first president. For many years he directed the Medicis Villa in Rome.

BLANCHE, JACQUES-ÉMILE

Born in Paris 1st February 1861. Died at Offranville in 1942. From his first exhibition, in 1882. almost until his death, he followed the worldly painter's career, painting the French and English celebrities of his time; Gide, Proust and Giraudoux were, among many others, his models for portraits which were done with great virtuosity, and are reminiscent of the English masters of the 17th century. An essayist and critic as well, he contributed to various artistic and poetic journals.

BÖCKLIN, ARNOLD

Born in Basel in 1837. Died at San Domenico, near Florence, 16th January 1901. After his artistic studies in Düsseldorf, he travelled in France and Belgium; then he became a teacher at the Weimar Academy before settling in Rome, in 1862. He escapes academicism by the brilliance of his intense colours.

BOLDINI, JEAN

Born at Ferrara 31st December 1845. Died in Paris 12th January 1931. After having studied in Florence for six years, and then in London around 1869, he went to Paris in 1872 and very quickly made a reputation there as a portraitist. A certain originality marks his expressive technique and, above all, an elegant virtuosity that makes him the historian of the worldly society of his time. There is something of Manet in his art, but adapted to suit the tastes of the ”gentry“.

BONINGTON, RICHARD PARKES

Born in Arnold (Nottingham) 25th October 1802. Died in London 23rd September 1828. His work is marked by a dual character, Romantic and Pre-Impressionist. As a small child he went to Calais where he had lessons with the water-colourist, Francia, which enabled him to play an important part in the new artistic movement. A friend of Delacroix, he learnt some useful lessons from the Italian painters whose work he went to study in Venice, about 1824.

BONNARD, PIERRE

Born at Fontenay-aux-Roses 3rd October 1867. Died at Cannet 23rd January 1947. Pierre Bonnard's life was not adventurous. His father was chief clerk at the Ministry of War and did not dream of having a painter in his family. Pierre Bonnard himself was not inspired by an irresistible call and it was after he had finished his law studies, in which he failed, that he obtained permission to try a new career by entering the École des Beaux-Arts et des Arts Decoratifs. At the Julian Academy he met Sérusier, Maurice Denis and Ranson; Gauguin was revealed to him by Sérusier and with his friends he formed the Nabis group, partly as a joke, partly out of sentiment. What the Impressionists had done for landscape, that is to say, making it possible to freeze the moment, to capture the atmosphere of the countryside, Bonnard did for interior scenes animated by silent characters. The first part of his work corresponds to a quiet intimacy, a tender pattern of grisailles; in his last years, on the other hand, he revealed the dazzling quality of a palette that was extremely colourful and astonishingly youthful.

BONNAT, LÉON-JOSEPH-FLORENTIN

Born at Bayonne 25th June 1833. Died in 1922. His portraits made him famous. Victor Hugo, Renan and Carnot did not disdain to pose for him. But he was misguided in neglecting large compositions in favour of them. After a long life, he bequeathed to his native town not only some rich collections but a museum.

BOUDIN, EUGÈNE

Born at Honfleur 13th July 1824. Died at Deauville 8th August 1898. Boudin was discovered in 1845 by Millet who, passing through Le Havre noticed the pictures shown by the young man in the window of his picture-frame shop. During his life, Boudin travelled a lot in Belgium, Brittany, the north of France, Paris, then Bordeaux, and later on the Côte d'Azur and Venice. With his friends, he was a member of the Impressionist group from the first exhibition, in 1874, and he too knew some years of poverty, but was quickly accepted by art lovers. In 1881, Durand-Ruel became his regular patron and, in 1883, organized an important exhibition for him. Boudin even won a gold medal at the Exposition Universelle of 1889. The sea is the almost exclusive theme of his pictures, with vast skies iridescent with the tenderest greys. Corot called him: " the king of skies".

BREITNER, GEORG HENDRIK

Born in Rotterdam 12th December 1857. Died in Amsterdam in 1923. First influenced by Van Gogh and the Naturalists (he was known as the Zola of Amsterdam) he painted popular scenes with social undertones, nudes, cavaliers; then his painting became more and more spatial and he devoted himself, above all, to landscape, using an Impressionist technique which added to a remarkable graphic quality. In 1886 he settled in Amsterdam, of which he painted a great many views which testify to his talent.

BROWN, FORD-MADOX

Born in Calais 16th April 1821. Died in London in October 1893. He displayed a precocious talent for drawing at the age of five, and his family spared no pains to develop his gifts. He travelled a lot, and was particularly sensitive to Flemish and German art, of which his work was to show a rather melodramatic trace, compensated by great power of expression. In 1848 Rossetti became his pupil and, from this meeting, Pre-Raphaelism was born.

BURNE-JONES, SIR EDWARD COLEY

Born in Birmingham 28th August 1833. Died in London 17th June 1898. He was reading theology at Oxford when he met Morris, heard Ruskin, and saw a drawing of Rossetti's-events that changed his

Pierre Bonnard
Nude before the Mirror. 1917
Private Collection, Paris

vocation. From 1855 to 1859, he studied painting in London with Rossetti, then travelled in Italy where the pictures of the Quattrocento taught him a lot. He also designed many tapestries for Morris. His career was a continuous success.

CAILLEBOTTE, GUSTAVE

Born in Paris 19th August 1848. Died at Gennevilliers 21st February 1894. A pupil of Bonnat, he soon left him to join the Impressionists, who were disapproved of at that time. He is less famous for his painting than for having assembled and bequeathed to the Louvre the finest Impressionist collection of his time.

CAROLUS-DURAN, CHARLES-ÉMILE

Born in Lille 4th July 1838. Died in Paris 18th February 1917. A painter and sculptor, he studied in Paris and Rome and also in Spain. The Evening Prayer was one of the first pictures he sent to the Salon; it was shown in 1866 and thereafter he quickly made a name as a portraitist. But this easy success sometimes led him into mere facility. His drawing often lacks science and accuracy, and his pictures often lack feeling.

CARRAND, LOUIS-HILAIRE

Born in Lyons 23rd August 1821. Died in Lyons 13th November 1899. To some extent a week-end artist he did his painting, considerable because of its quantity, during the leisure hours that his work as a copy-clerk left him. Poverty often obliged him to use both sides of a canvas or a piece of pasteboard. Nature was his real master, apart from the landscape-painter, Nicolas Fonville, who gave him lessons for two years.

CARRIÈRE, EUGÈNE

Born at Gournay (Seine-et-Oise) in 1849. Died in Paris in 1906. He can be considered as the first great Intimist of his time; his art preserved something of the pictures of Georges de La Tour and as a novice he copied him tirelessly; yet he combined a very strong personality with technical perfection. In his portraits, expressive characterization animates the faces which seem to surge out of a mist (his portrait of Verlaine, for example). His work, rich in feeling, exalts the home, the family, maternal love.

CASSATT, MARY

Born in Pittsburgh (Pennsylvania) in 1845. Died at Mesnil-Beaufresne (Oise) 14th June 1927. Through her father, she descended from a Frenchman who had emigrated to Holland in 1662, before taking refuge in the United States. At the age of twenty-three, she decided to devote herself exclusively to painting and joined the Impressionists; in 1879 she took part in their fourth exhibition, in the Avenue de l'Opera. Guided by Degas, she adopted a firm style of drawing and brilliant colours.

CÉZANNE, PAUL

Born in Aix-en-Provence 19th January 1839. Died there 22nd October 1906. Like all young men of good family (his father was a banker in Aix-en-Provence) Cézanne was destined for a professional career and was accordingly enrolled in the law faculty of Aix-en-Provence. But he showed little enthusiasm for it and obtained permission to study fine arts at the same time. In 1861 he even managed to study painting in Paris where his friend, Émile Zola, had arrived a year earlier. He attended the Swiss Academy, where he met Guillaumin and Pissarro. After a new attempt at a reasonable life, in Aix, where he accepted a job in his father's bank, he returned to his friends in Paris, Bazille, Renoir, Monet, Sisley, and joined their group in Gleyre's studio. His attempt to enter the École des Beaux-Arts ended in failure but did not discourage him any more than the fact of being refused by the selection committee of the Salon, to whom he regularly submitted his work. At that time he was painting still lifes, portraits and other composition with a rough, almost clumsy technique, heavy with impastos. During the war, he took refuge in l'Estaque, near Marseilles, and returned to Paris when the war was over. Under Pissarro's influence, he turned to the open air and painted landscapes according to Nature, in the vicinity of Pontoise, following a technique that was very close to that of the Impressionists. He faced the public for the first time at the Exhibition of 1874 and made the visitors laugh. For a very long time the public was hostile to his art and Cézanne preferred to return to Aix rather than make any concessions to them. Even his friend, Émile Zola, completely misunderstood him and modelled the character of Claudio Lautier, failed painter, hero of the novel entitled *l'Oeuvre*, on him. It was only towards 1900 that the importance of Cézanne's painting began to be appreciated. Of course, a number of painters, notably Gauguin, had appreciated his qualities well before, but he was so fundamentally opposed to Impressionism that he only asserted himself when he felt the need to defend himself against the movement. All the great movements in painting, after 1900 and for more than half a century, in France and abroad, were to turn to Cézanne and the austere discipline with which he opposed the brilliant facility of his Impressionist friends.

CONSTABLE, JOHN

Born at East Bergholt in 1776. Died in London in 1837. The development of his personality was slow because he only became fully conscious of it towards the age of forty. Thereafter he asserted himself and opened the way to the modern landscape-painters; his landscapes, in which he caught, better than anyone, the essence of the English countryside in all its aspects, were revolutionary not only in England but also in France, where one of the pictures he sent to the Salon of 1824 (The Haycart Crossing a Ford) was a revelation that was to have a decisive influence on the Barbizon School. (Between 1824 and 1826, 27 of his works were shown in Paris).

CORINTH, LOVIS

Born at Tapiau (East Prussia) 21st June 1858. Died in 1925. Between 1884 and 1887 he studied in Paris at the Julian Academy and this stay was to have a decisive influence on the very personal style of his work. He painted portraits, still lifes, and mythological and religious scenes.

COROT, JEAN-BAPTISTE

Born in Paris 16th July 1796. Died at Ville d'Avray 22nd February 1875. One could not sum up Corot's character better than by quoting from his bio-

Eugène-Louis Boudin The Canal at Brussels. 1871
Mrs. Thelma Cazalet-Keir's Collection, London

grapher, Alfred Robaut: " Did he not have, in equal parts, the good qualities of his father and his mother? His father... always cheerful and happy with his lot, only carrying small sums of money about with him, counted in advance, and carefully prepared for each person that he had to see; his mother, on the other hand, less attentive to small things, a woman of high tastes, in short, very artistic in her way". She kept a fashion shop in the Rue du Bac, opposite the Pont Royal. These reasonable parents had wanted to see their son become a good business man; after several fruitless tries, they resigned themselves to giving him a small allowance to enable him to paint and draw, for he was no good at anything else. Corot was first advised by the painter, Michallon, then by Victor Bertin. In 1825 he went on his first trip to Italy, exhibited for the first time at the Salon of 1827, and returned to France in 1828. He was to go back to Italy in 1834 and in 1843

but, from his first stay, this country left its mark on him and, in contact with Nature, he achieved a mastery and a style that he was not to surpass, even when the landscape of Ile-de-France suggested less austere harmonies to him – harmonies he was to appreciate and whose charms he was to reproduce. In every case, as much in the Italian landscapes standing out in the limpid air as in those he painted in France that were softened by mist, Corot remained at the service of Nature and believed in reproducing it faithfully although he imposed a very pure classical style on it. One finds the same mixture of grandeur and simplicity in his portraits which had no success during his lifetime but which, by common consent, are now considered among the finest works of the 19th century. Modesty was an essential trait of Corot's and marks the least important of his works, just as his extreme generosity marked the whole of his life.

COTMAN, JOHN SELL

Born in Norwich 16th May 1782. Died in London 24th July 1842. A painter of landscapes and, above all, of seascapes, a water-colourist and architectural engraver (he is particularly well known for the hundred very remarkable plates he did of the ancient architecture of Normandy, which were published in 1822). Around 1800 he went to London, where he met Turner. With Crome, he was one of the finest artists of the Norwich School. His art is characterized by a simplicity of forms that is almost Chinese, but it is a simplicity adorned in the richest colours.

COURBET, GUSTAVE

Born at Ornans (Doubs) 10th June 1819. Died at La Tour de Peilz 31st December 1877. All Courbet's work is imbued with his peasant origins, in spite of the time he spent at the Ornans seminary and at the Besançon Lycée, in spite of his intention to study Law in Paris. It really seems that Courbet wanted to be a painter in order to give material reality to the pleasure he took in looking at Nature. He spreads colour over the canvas with the essential joy of a gourmand; the foliage of a forest, the water of a cascade, the rocks of a cliff, the body of a woman, are means of seizing throbbing life; even Courbet's political attitudes were a kind of physical expansion, a glow of life and liberty, and not a philosophical standpoint, thought out in relation to Man's destiny. His first canvasses show evident signs of the Romantic influence, and the Realism of his later work was not a denial of his early work but rather a logical development, a way of going further in affirming his passion for life more violently. Because of their titles, his contemporaries had serious reservations about his work. Pictures like *The Burial at Ornans*, *The Studio*, *The Stone-Breakers* and *Coming Back from the Lecture* were discussed as much for their character as for their technique. Doubtless his work is not without political under-tones, but these are primarily the expression of a passionate, impulsive temperament. In 1855, *The Studio* having been refused by the selection committee of the Exposition Universelle, Courbet organized in a hovel, in the Place de l'Alma, an exhibition of his own work which affirmed his position as a rebel. His very scholarly techinique could not be considered as a prelude to Impressionism, but he was largely responsible for the liberation of the artist from academic rules, for the refusal to submit to worldly conventions, and the love of independence that was to lead

him, after the 1870 War, to take part in the extremist movements. The government of Thiers wanted to hold him responsible for the destruction of the Vendôme Column and he was not only condemned to imprisonment, but also forced to pay a heavy fine for the repair of the monument. Faced with so much hostility, Courbet had to leave France to find some peace in Switzerland.

COUSTURIER, LUCIE

Born in Paris 19th December 1876. Died in Paris 16th June 1925. She played an important role in the Neo-Impressionist group, as much through her writings as her paintings. A pupil of Signac, and a passionate admirer of Seurat, she showed a great interest in colonial art. From 1906 to 1913, she exhibited at the Salon de la Libre Esthétique, Brussels.

CROME, JOHN ("Old Crome")

Born in Norwich 22nd December 1768. Died there 22nd April 1821. Had a difficult start in life, for he had to earn his living from the age of twelve. Working as a messenger, he met Sir William Beechey who allowed him to copy the works of Flemish and Dutch masters in his collection. And so the young boy learnt his art. In 1803 he founded the "Norwich Society of Artists"; from 1805 onwards, their exhibitions launched one of the finest schools of landscape-painters in England. It is to be noted, however, that Crome never painted outdoors but did all his work in his studio.

CROSS, HENRY-EDMOND

Born at Douai 20th May 1856. Died at Saint-Clair, near Lavandou (Var), 16th May 1910. He painted in sombre colours when he worked in Bonvin's studio (Bonvin made him change his name from Delacroix to Cross. In 1884 he suddenly brightened his palette and began to utilise the division of colours. He first laid on dashes of white and then glazed them over with colours. After 1908 he abandoned systematic Pointillism and adopted a freer style, while remaining much more under the influence of Neo-Impressionism than he believed.

DAUBIGNY, CHARLES-FRANÇOIS

Born in Paris 15th February 1817. Died 19th February 1878. Studied with his father, who was a

Honoré Daumier The Refugees.
Petit Palais, Paris

painter. At the age of seventeen, after a visit to Rome, he became a picture-restorer at the Musée du Louvre and then entered the house of Delaroche, the historical painter. After 1844 his predilection for painting water (ponds, streams, rivers) asserted itself and enabled him to express the quiet harmony of atmosphere and, at the same time, the most secret stirrings of the spirit. He was to live for several years on "le Bottin", a barge-studio that he had specially built.

His influence can be seen in Jongkind, Boudin, Courbet, Lépine, etc.

DAUMIER, HONORÉ

Born in Marseilles 26th February 1808. Died at Valmondois 11th February 1879. With his rare skill as a draughtsman, with all the qualities of heart and mind, but without riches, Daumier, a great artist, could not give all he was capable of since, in order to earn his living, he had to supply editors with a constant stream of humorous drawings and could not devote all the time he would have liked to painting. His work nevertheless comprises some two hundred pictures, but this is very little compared with the four thousand lithographs that were published in the various journals for which he worked until the day his sight prevented it. For Daumier this would have meant the most wretched and unjust poverty if it had not been for the watchful friendship of Corot who, to save his friend, bought the house where he was living and offered it to him (1868). His first caricatures – of commissioned portraits – were done in about 1830, engraved figurines that gave Philipon the idea of asking him for some lithographs to publish in his journal "*La Caricature*" and then in "*Charivari*". Daumier's spirited satire stirred up serious enmity in goverment circles (in 1832 he was arrested for a caricature against Louis Philippe); but in spite of all this bullying, he was to go on throughout his life castigating the follies of his age with a violence that stemmed from a desire for justice and not from ill-nature.

DEGAS, EDGAR

Born in Paris 19th July 1834. Died there 27th September 1917. Degas, the son of a banker, entered the École des Beaux-Arts in 1855, having already begun studying Law. His teacher was Lamothe, who could only confirm his admiration for Ingres, some of whose drawings he had been able to see at the house of Madame Valpincon, a friend of the family.

A visit to Italy in 1856 (he met Gustave Moreau and Léon Bonnat there, and met Elie Delaunay again), and a familiarity with the Musée du Louvre – these enabled him to acquire a solid Classical background. Some almost academic compositions date from this period (*Spartan Girls Wrestling, Semiramis Building a City, The Poor of Orleans*) but at the same time Degas' taste for everyday scenes, realistic portraits and a number of racing pictures, prove his desire to escape conventions and capture the image of the daily life about him. Doubtless it was this non-conformism that enabled him to fit into the group from which Impressionism was to emerge in 1874. But he served these ideas with a technique that was very different from that of the other young artists; he remained faithful to his learning and would not accept work that appeared improvised or fortuitous. Above all, he marks himself off from them by his choice of subjects and by the fact that, no matter what his theme, he always gives first place to Man who, with the others, is treated much more as an accessory. Whether it be in the portraits, the dancing scenes, the washer-woman or milliner series, the pictures inspired by the theatre, or nude women bathing or dressing, what counts is the human face, or body. One knows of hardly any landscapes.

Moreover, Degas loved very contrived work, artificial and, in particular, unusual placings, with portraits off centre, the foregrounds very important. Thus, a conception of space, which was to be rediscovered many years later in photography and especially in the cinema, made Degas an unwitting forerunner in a domain where no one thought art would intervene.

DENIS, MAURICE

Born at Grandville 25th November 1870. Died in an accident in Paris 13th November 1943. He remains one of the artists who best learnt the lesson of liberty and discipline given by Gauguin at Pont-Aven; for several years he searched for a path that would enable him to put aside Academicism and find a purer Classicism; Gauguin's example was to supply him with a chance to do this. After 1890 he became the spokesman of the Pont-Aven group, and then of the Nabis, and although his art did not always correspond to the theories that he formulated, (he held an important place and exercised some in-

fluence) before the appearance of the Fauve and Cubist movements. A mystic, he used the best of his talent in reviving Catholic art; and with Georges Desvallières he founded the Studio of Sacred Art. He was one of the founders of the Salon d'Automne, where he succeeded in having a religious art section opened.

DIAZ, DE LA PEÑA NARCISSE-VIRGILE

Born in Bordeaux 20th August 1807. Died at Menton 18th November 1876. This colourist, who influenced modern art more than one imagines, had a most romantic life: the son of Spanish emigrants, he became an orphan at the age of ten and was cared for by a Protestant pastor. At fifteen he was bitten by a snake and had his right leg amputated. His love of Nature was not lessened by this – far from it. After an apprenticeship as a painter of porcelain, he took part in the Salon of 1831 and installed himself at Barbizon toward the age of thirty. His art, which flowed entirely from inspiration, was already a pursuit of the joy of colours, free of preoccupation with the subject.

EAKINS, THOMAS

Born in Philadelphia 25th 1844. Died there in 1916. A painter and sculptor, he was particularly interested in sporting subjects. He studied painting in Paris with Bonnat and Gérôme, and sculpture, with Dumont.

EILSHEMIUS, LOUIS MICHEL

Born in the State of New York in 1864. Died in 1942. Although he studied in Paris at the Julian Academy, he was a representative painter of the American School. One can see some of his work in the Philipps Memorial Gallery of Washington, D.C.

ENSOR, JAMES

Born at Ostend 13th April 1860. Died there in 1949. From the time of his first exhibition in 1881, at the Chrysalide, the strange, intense light that bathes his pictures became noticeable; but *Woman with a Retroussé Nose (1870)* should be considered his real debut as a painter. His talent expressed itself in two ways, one realistic, the other visionary, and he sometimes united them in one picture. His

Oyster Eater (*1882*) was the first luminous painting done in Belgium. He also introduced new themes into painting – skeletons and carnivals. *Christ's Entry into Brussels* (*1888*) marks an essential stage in this artist's development.

EVENEPOEL, HENRI-JACQUES-ÉDOUARD

Born in Nice 4th October 1872. Died in Paris 27th December 1899. It was in the last months of his short career that he accomplished the most important part of his work. He was a pupil of Gustave Moreau in Paris, and with his careful technique he made elegant use of greys, pinks and ochres. One of his pictures is *The Spaniard in Paris*.

FANTIN-LATOUR, IGNACE-HENRI-JEAN-THÉODORE

Born at Grenoble 14th January 1836. Died at Buré (Orne) 25th August 1904. The son of a painter, he first studied with his father and then entered the École des Beaux-Arts in 1854. It was not until 1870 that his picture, *A Studio at Batignolles* was noticed and brought him reward. From the beginning he had established himself as a refined draughtsman and colourist. A music-lover, he tried to transcribe his musical feelings into pastels and lithographs.

FATTORI, GIOVANNI

Born at Livorno 25th October 1825. Died in Florence 30th August 1908. When he followed his inspiration, he achieved great mastery; the way in which he delimits forms while conserving their weight and bathing them in a sharp, limpid light, merits him the appellation bestowed on him by his contemporaries: "An idiot of a genius". After 1847 he worked in Florence, frequenting the Michelangelo cafe and belonging to the Macchiaioli movement, a group of Italian painters who used the Tachist technique and in which he held an important place.

Having won, in 1861, the first prize in a competition for painters of battle-scenes, he became the foremost Italian military painter.

FORAIN, JEAN-LOUIS

Born at Reims 23rd October 1852. Died in Paris 11th July 1931. He had a difficult start, but the foundation of "*Courrier Français*" and, later, "*Rire*" enabled him to exploit his extraordinary powers of observation and expression, in drawings that were often cruelly ironical. He exhibited with the Impressionists twice, but his sombre paintings, swept with crude streaks of luminous colour, have neither the lyricism nor the force of his drawings.

GAUGUIN, PAUL

Born in Paris 7th June 1848. Died at Atouana, La Dominique (Marquesas Isles) 8th May 1903. It is necessary once again to summarise Gauguin's life, so many times documented, commented upon and distorted. Through his maternal grandmother, Flora Trista, he descended from a Spanish family settled in Peru where one of his uncles was Viceroy. His early childhood – from three to seven – was spent in Lima. He then returned to France, a pilot's apprentice in the Merchant Navy at the age of seventeen, joined a crew at the age of twenty, returned to civilian life after the 1870-71 War, took a job with a stock-broker in Paris and in 1873 married a Danish girl by whom he soon had five children. In 1883 he gave up his speculations (perhaps because he was forced to do so by a financial crash) and from then on, saw no other solution than to devote himself to painting, which until then had been an agreeable pastime. His quiet bourgeois life was at an end; his dramatic life as an artist began and he was immediately beset by material problems. First he had to leave the little house with studio and garden in rue Carcel, and seek a less burdensome life in the provinces – there was a brief stay in Rouen before leaving with his family for Copenaghen, where his wife hoped to find a friendly atmosphere that would facilitate the enterprises of a husband by now becoming incomprehensible. With his rather eccentric personality he felt ill at ease in this prudent Lutheran milieu, which became daily more alien, not to say hostile. His return to France in 1885 marked the beginning of his years of great poverty. Intermittent stays in Paris and Brittany, interrupted by a few months in Martinique in 1887 and, at the end of the year 1888, in Arles with Van Gogh (where a mutual friendship blazed up into drama) – these served to convince Gauguin of his dissatisfaction with the world around him.

In 1891 he went to Tahiti to pursue his ideal of passion and purity among more primitive tribes. Poverty and illness accompanied him; his return to France between 1883 and 1885 was short-lived; he found confirmation there of the rift between him and the era.

His last stay in Brittany ended in a brawl with some sailors who smashed his ankle with kicks from their wooden clogs – an injury from which he was to suffer for the rest of his life. He died in 1903, on one of the Marquesas Isles.

For many years he had definitely been at odds with our civilization, harassed by local authorities, gendarmes, missionaries and governors, with whom he was in perpetual conflict in defence of the natives.

GERVEX, HENRI

Born in Paris in 1852. Died 7th June 1929. A friend of Renoir's, he was nevertheless alarmed at the boldness of Impressionism and preferred a more Classical art – which brought him numerous official commissions, both in France and abroad. He painted faithful portraits, notably one of Napoleon III and another of Doctor Péan.

GUIGOU, PAUL-ÉMILE

Born at Villars, near Apt (Vaucluse) 15th February 1834. Died in Paris 21st December 1871. Mistral said of him: « He painted a faithful and lasting portrait of his birth-place". In fact, he did capture Provence in his small canvasses (where he was more at his ease than in large paintings); he did not interpret, but transcribed with fervour, and his landscapes of the Durance valley are very intimate.

GUILLAUMIN, JEAN-BAPTISTE-ARMAND

Born in Paris 15th February 1841. Died 26th June 1927. While working in commerce and later for the Paris-Orléans Railway Company, he spent his leisure hours painting. In 1863 there occurred the decisive meeting with Pissarro, at the Swiss Academy. In spite of the faint enthusiasm of Degas and Monet, who did not appreciate his art, he took part in six of the eight Impressionist exhibitions and attended the meetings at the café Guerbois.

Towards 1904 he became interested in Fauvism. After 1892 he was able to devote himself exclusively to painting, thanks to a prize won in the draw for the Crédit Foncier.

GUYS, CONSTANTIN-ERNEST-ADOLPHE-HYACINTHE

Born at Flessingue (Holland) 3rd December 1805. Died in Paris in 1892. A draughtsman with a rapid, telling line, in his early days he was sent to the Crimea by the Illustrated London News as their war correspondent. He loved painting scenes of fashionable life – parades, dancers, fêtes. No oil painting seems to exist by Guys. During the last year of his life, he even used colour only with great discretion. His style is one of the most expressive and individual of the 19th century, and Baudelaire was his enthusiastic panegyrist.

HARPIGNIES, HENRI-JOSEPH

Born at Valenciennes 28th July 1819. Died at Saint-Privé (Yonne) 28th August 1916. He was to the Barbizon School what Guillaumin was to be to Impressionism. A long list of awards testifies to the merits of his upright life, which he devoted to the Arts, and his deeply sincere love of Nature, which he could paint in all her moods and aspects. Yet he was a late-comer to painting, having begun as a commercial traveller, and the first picture he sent to the Salon, *View of Capri*, dates from 1853.

HÉBERT, ANTOINE-AUGUSTE-ERNEST

Born in Grenoble 3rd November 1817. Died at La Tronche, near Grenoble, 5th November 1908. Born of a bourgeois family, he managed to study painting and Law simultaneously and pursued these studies to a successful end: in the same year he won the Prix de Rome, and became a lawyer. But it was to painting that he dedicated his life, and he holds an important place among the artists of his time; he is even one of the most authoritative representatives of the Classical tradition. He painted a great number of excellent portaits, but his works also includes some landscapes which are less known but testify to the interest he took in the observation of Nature.

HENNER, JEAN-JACQUES

Born at Berwiller (upper Rhine) 5th March 1829. Died 23rd July 1905. In Alsace, at the age of twelve he began taking lessons. He acquired a wide cultural backround. Berwiller is not far from Basel, and Henner often went there to admire the work of Holbein. He won the Prix de Rome in 1858. A member of the Institut in 1889, his success crowned a life of patient, persevering effort. His art sought to give expression to high aspirations through means that were sometimes honest to the point of naïveté.

HODLER FERDINAND

Born in Bern 14th March 1853. Died in Geneva 19th May 1918. After a long career in the course of which he tried every genre (portrait, landscape, historical painting, etc.), Hodler did not become famous and see his talent recognised by his contemporaries until the exhibition of the Secession of Vienna in 1904. Attracted by luminous colours and Impressionist principles towards 1890, he still remained an architect of composition and a draughtsman rather than a colourist.

HOMER, WINSLOW

Born in Boston 24th February 1836. Died at Scaboro 29th September 1910. Considered one of the great masters of the American School, his apprenticeship was that of a lithographer. He took part in the Universal Exhibition of 1867 and in that of 1900 (where he won a medal). After a stay in England in 1881-82, he modified his style which, both Romantic and Realistic, became broader and assumed dazzling colours.

HUNT, WILLIAM HOLMAN

Born in London 2nd April 1827. Died there 7th September 1910. He was eighteen when he first exhibited at the Royal Academy, in 1845. He very soon joined up with Ford Madox Brown and Rossetti and became one of the most important figures in the Pre-Raphaelite movement. At first an historical painter, after a visit to Palestine to see the background of Christ's life, his work became steeped in Christian symbolism.

ISRAELS, ISAAC

Born in Amsterdam 3rd February 1865. Died at Leiden in 1934. At first he was deeply influenced by his father, the well-known painter Joseph Israel.

Johann Jongkind Landscape with Windmill
Private Collection, Paris

Around 1882 the reading of Zola's "Germinal" led him to visit Charleroi in order to depict the life of the workers there. Later, he painted scenes of elegant London life, when his style had changed after meeting Toulouse-Lautrec and imbibing Impressionism in Paris (from 1903 to 1914). He also left a great number of pastels, water-colours, lithographs and etchings.

JONGKIND JOHANN BARTHOLD

Born at Latrop, near Rotterdam, 3rd June 1819. Died in Grenoble 9th February 1891. Jongkind was not only a forerunner of the Impressionists: through his life, in which women and drink played a tragic role, he also heralded the "possessed painters" and provided the first chapter of the martyrdom of modern art. Several friends tried to save him from this wretched fate: in 1846 Isabey took him to Paris, tried several times to help him, and introduced him to the landscapes at the mouth of the Seine and the

Normandy beaches; but Jongkind was not to escape his wild life. The painters, Sano and Cals, were among others who tried to help him. His poverty ceased for a time when Madame Fesser, a Dutch art teacher, succeeded in putting some order into his life; but during the last years, when he was settled in Côte-St-André, between Lyons and Grenoble, he sank back into alcoholism and finished his days in a lunatic asylum in Grenoble.

KLIMT, GUSTAV

Born in Vienna 14th July 1862. Died there 6th February 1918. A Viennese at heart, he rarely left his native city, where he studied and spent his whole career as a painter. Influenced by Toorop, Khnoopf and Japanese painting, he created a personal style in which one finds echoes of Toulouse-Lautrec and Gauguin, Munch and Nolde. An active representative of Jugendstil, he founded the Secession of Vienna In 1897.

190

LAURENT, ERNEST-JOSEPH

Born in Paris 8th June 1859. Died at Bièvres 25th June 1929. Winner of the Prix de Rome in 1889, his work gained numerous awards and was influenced in turns by official art and by the Neo-Impressionism of his friend Seurat. He used Pointillism for soft blurred effects. Portraits comprise an important part of his work.

LEBOURG, ALBERT-CHARLES

Born at Montfort-sur-Risle (Eure) 1st February 1849. Died in Rouen 7th January 1928. He worked with an architect in Rouen, before attending the École des Beaux-Arts. From 1872 to 1877 he taught in Algiers. Without knowing the Impressionists, he adopted a technique there which put him close to them. He went back to Paris in 1877 and exhibited with them in 1878 – which did not prevent him from taking part in the exhibitions of the Salon de la Nationale from the time of its foundation in 1890.

LEIBL, WILHELM-MARIA-HUBERTUS

Born in Cologne 23rd October 1844. Died at Wurtzbourg 4th December 1900. A painter and engraver, he was influenced by Courbet's style. During the 90's he taught, in Munich, those who were later to create in that city the most important movements in modern German painting.

LEMMEN, GEORGES

Born at Scharbeek in 1865. Died at Uccle 5th May 1916. An admirer of Van Rysselberghe, his work was steeped in Intimism and strongly influenced by French Impressionism. Three of his works are in the Musée de Bruxelles: *The Nursery, The Reading and Sewing*.

LÉPINE, STANISLAS-VICTOR-ÉDOUARD

Born at Caen 3rd October 1835. Died in Paris 28th September 1892. He was a pupil of Corot, from whom he inherited a great simplicity and sincerity of expression; from Jongkind, whom he admired, he acquired ease in rendering the depth of the sky or the limpidity of water.
His painting does not lend itself to analysis, but is made simply for the pleasure of the viewer.

LE SIDANER, HENRI-EUGÈNE-AUGUSTIN

Born in Port Louis, Mauritius, 7th August 1862. Died in 1939. His art lies between that of the Neo-Impressionists and that of Eugène Carrière. He adopted the technique of painting in short strokes, in order to express the soft intimacy of interiors or the tenderness of calm landscapes. He often sought to catch the fleeting restlessness of twilight.

LIEBERMANN, MAX

Born in Berlin 20th July 1847. Died in 1935. He began painting at the age of twenty-one. His first big picture, *The Goose Pluckers*, made him famous; he was twenty-six. His Realistic work is marked by Millet's influence. Later on he gradually brought light into his palette and turned to less austere subjects. He stopped painting in 1880, but was also an engraver and writer.

LUCE, MAXIMILIEN

Born in Paris 13th March 1858. Died there 6th February 1941. His life was difficult and toilsome. After a childhood in which poverty and local drama played their part, he learnt wood-engraving and it was not until 1876 that he was able to paint his first complete canvas, *The Garden of Grand-Montrouge*. Maximilien Luce was a keen observer of Nature, and his landscapes are remarkable; those of the Pointillist period should not, however, lead us to neglect those of Rolleboise that he painted after shaking off the disciplines of Neo-Impressionism (from 1908 onwards).

MACKE, AUGUST

Born at Meschede (Ruhr) 3rd January 1887. Died at Perthes in Champagne on September 26, 1914. A painter, he also studied theatre decoration and décor. In 1911 he founded in Munich the "Blaue Reiter" with Kandinsky and Franz Marc. In 1914 he accompanied Paul Klee on the famous visit to Tunisia when Klee discovered the sources and laws of colour.

MANET, ÉDOUARD

Born in Paris 23rd January 1832. Died there 30th April 1883. Manet's parents (his father was head of the Lord Chancellor's office, and later a court adviser; his mother the daughter of one of Napoleon's diplomatic agents) would have liked to see their son become a magistrate. After a brief and unfruitful period in the navy, he was allowed to follow the courses given by the shrewd Thomas Couture (1849); in spite of inevitable disagreements, he persevered for several years although the lessons that he had were probably less valuable than his numerous visits to the Louvre, or his visits to Italy, Germany, Holland and, later, Spain (1865). The first picture he sent to the Salon, in 1861, *Lola of Valence*, was noticed by Baudelaire. The second, *Dejeuner sur l'herbe*, submitted in 1863, was rejected; Manet sent it to the Salon des Refusés, where it caused a scandal. There was a still greater scandal at the Salon of 1865 with *Olympia*. In 1867 he organised an exhibition of fifty of his paintings in a hovel similar to Courbet's, and near the Universal Exhibition, and thus became, unintentionally, an example of independence and soon the leader of a school of painting, too. The supporters of Realism and Naturalism did not stint him in their encouragement. Zola sided with him, and when young artists wanted to escape Academicism, to paint in the open air with luminous colours, it was to him that they turned although he had never agreed to take part in an Impressionist exhibition, not even the first. After a stay in Argenteuil with Claude Monet in 1874, Manet adopted a lighter palette but without renouncing black, a colour which he used with rare mastery and great elegance. In spite of the alternate rejections and acceptances of the Salon selection committee, his art gained a footing little by little: in 1880 he won a second prize, and in 1882, through his friend Antonin Proust, then Minister of Fine Arts, he received the Légion d'Honneur. His large output has affinities with the work of more conventional artists such as Stevens, Tissot, Gervex, Roll and also Jacques-Emile Blanche and Forain. Thus Manet's work, like his life, has a dual aspect, making the man of the world a revolutionary in spite of himself.

MARTIN, HENRI-JEAN-GUILLAUME ("Henri-Martin")

Born in Toulouse 5th August 1860. Died in Paris in November 1943. In 1879 he began studying with J.P. Laurens in Paris, but it was during a visit to Italy in 1885 that he discovered his real self and adopted a special technique which enabled him to express the intensity of his poetic feelings. From then on he used short strokes, detached and parallel, which gave his canvasses a hazy atmosphere.

His most important mural is the one he did for the Capitol of Toulouse.

MENZEL, ADOLF-FRIEDRICH-ERDMANN

Born at Breslau 8th December 1815. Died in Berlin 9th February 1905. In both his choice of subjects and his technique he is near the Realism of Courbet. Some forty of his pictures and several thousand engravings and drawings are in the National Gallery of Berlin.

MILLAIS, SIR JOHN EVERETT

Born in Southampton 8th June 1829. Died in London 13th August 1896. A painter of landscape, genre and historical scenes, but above all, an excellent portraitist, he was also remarkably precocious: he attended courses at the Royal Academy at the age of eleven. At fourteen he won a silver medal, at eighteen a gold medal; and at twenty, breaking with Academicism, he linked up with Ruskin and became the leader of the Pre-Raphaelites.

MILLET, JEAN-FRANÇOIS

Born at Gruchy, in the commune of Gréville, not far from Cherbourg, 4th October 1814. Died at Barbizon 20th January 1875. Millet made a brilliant start for, considered an infant prodigy by his family, and having obtained a grant from the township of Cherbourg to go and work in Paris, he was soon encouraged by his teacher at the École des Beaux-Arts, the painter Paul Delaroche; but it was to the Louvre, above all, that Millet went in search of lessons. His art quickly grew away from current tastes. The first pictures he sent to the Salon, in 1840, were not a great success and certain of them were even rejected. His simple life became a difficult life. His love of Nature, more and more in evidence, led him away from Romantic images and, at the same time, from Academicism. In order to live he had to take on menial work like painting signboards, and throughout his life he was to accept an extremely modest existence so as to remain faithful to his ideas, his scruples. One knows him best for his moving images of peasant life, painted in humility; one forgets too easily that he left some very remarkable portraits, painted with vigour and steeped with that warm humanity that one finds in all his work. In 1848 he settled in Barbizon where he stayed until the end of his life.

Claude Monet Regatta at Argenteuil. 1874
Musée du Louvre, Paris

MONET, CLAUDE

Born in Paris 14th November 1840. Died at Giverny 6th December 1926. Boudin, whose pictures Millet had noticed in a stationer's window in Le Havre, did exactly the same some ten years later for Monet, who was showing some caricatures in the window of a bookshop in Le Havre. Boudin prevailed on the young man to paint some landscapes and, in 1856, arranged for him to exhibit with him in Rouen. In 1857 Monet went to Paris and met Pissarro at the Swiss Academy. He went to Algeria on military service, returned in 1862, and joined Gleyre's studio where he met Sisley, Bazille and Renoir, with whom he left some months later for the Forest of Fontainebleau. An exhibition of Manet's at the home of Martinet was a revelation to him. He met Jongkind at Honfleur in 1865 and painted on the Normandy beaches. Some pictures with people in them also date from this period: *Le Dejeuner sur l'herbe, The Woman in a Green Dress, Women in a Garden* and *Le Dejeuner dans un interieur.*

Experiments not to be repeated for, in the following years, Monet was to paint only landscapes and a few still lifes. In London in 1870 he met Pissarro again and made the acquaintance of Durand-Ruel, who after the war was to become the Impressionists' chief salesman. The landscapes of the Seine Valley have an important place in all his work, although he travelled a lot along the Mediterranean coast (where he went for the first time in 1883 with Renoir), in Brittany, in Creuse and also outside France, in Holland, in Italy (he brought an important series of pictures back from Venice in 1908), to London, where he returned in 1891, and in Norway. But he always returned to Giverny, in Eure, where he settled in 1881 and where he finished his days, at once famous and somewhat forgotten, for after having known the most complete triumph, Impressionism was vigorously attacked by the younger generation, who wanted to escape from it and assert their independence. However, by a curious twist of fate, Claude Monet today again enjoys the epithet "modern" and support from among the young.

Unacademic painters find magnificent examples in his work and especially in the "Nympheas" series, which he painted untiringly in his garden at Giverny during the last years of his life. The other series on Rouen Cathedral, the bridges of London, Venice, hay-ricks and poplars, are like musical variations on a theme and constitute a prelude to the quest that was going on for the expression, over and beyond the subject, of a way of living and feeling.

MONTICELLI, ADOLPHE-JOSEPH-THOMAS

Born in Marseilles 16th October 1824. Died there 29th June 1886. At the age of twenty-two he gave up his work as a chemist in order to join Delaroche's studio, in Paris; but the Louvre was to be his real teacher.

At first he painted sparkling Romantic pictures, which won the admiration not only of masters like Delacroix but also that of the public (the Emperor was one of his first buyers); back in Marseilles after 1870, he adopted a more austere, difficult style, conserving his Impressionism through a light that fascinated Van Gogh.

MOREAU, GUSTAVE

Born in Paris 6th April 1826. Died there 18th April 1898. He had a very individual conception of colour and form, which he expressed in pictures that are full of curious details, and in gouaches or water-colours which testify to a keen feeling for painting. His chief claim to glory is doubtless the fact that he was the understanding teacher of those who became the Fauves – Matisse, Rouault, Marquet – and that he was a forerunner of Surrealism.

MORISOT, BERTHE

Born at Bourges 14th January 1841. Died in Paris 2nd March 1895. This artist did not have to undergo the material hardships of other painters but her art is as affirmative as theirs, as free. She led an untroubled life: her father, Prefect of Cher when she was born, did not object to her leanings; he very soon arranged for her to have lessons with Guichard, a painter from Lyons, who introduced her to Corot. Her parents willingly received artists at their house; she had already met Fantin-Latour and Manet at the Louvre. Jongkind gave her lessons in water-colour technique. She was accepted by the Salon of 1865 and it was out of preference, not in spite of it, that she took part in the 1874 Exhibition, where she received one of the rare commendations. At the sale that took place the following year, it was one of her canvases that fetched the highest price – 490 francs. She was very attached to Manet, both because of his art and his family life. In fact, in 1874 she married Eugène Manet, the painter's brother. Edouard did several portraits of him, notably in the picture entitled " Le Balcon " (1868). She brought a very personal note of femininity to Impressionism, of which one could find no equivalent in the land-scape-painters, Monet, Sisley or Pissarro (the human figure is nearly always absent in their work) or in Degas or Cézanne (they looked on women unfavourably) or in Renoir who, with his happy sensuality, saw women as beautiful animals.

MORRIS, WILLIAM

Born at Walthamstow (Essex) 24th March 1834. Died in London 3rd October 1896. Born into a rich family, he first thought of entering the clergy. During the course of his theological studies at Oxford, he became the intimate friend of Burne Jones, Ruskin's disciple, and took an interest in the plastic arts. He extended the Pre-Raphaelite movement, making it embrace all forms of decoration. His artistic activity always went hand in hand with his social and Christian work. Before all else a decorator, he founded his own furniture business. He also took an interest in de luxe printing and, in all his activities, had a considerable influence.

MUNCH, EDOUARD

Born at Loyten (Southern Norway) 12th December 1863. Died at Ekely 23rd January 1944. His " Sick Child ", which dates from as early as 1885, carries the personality of an artist of sure talent, master of his technique and the theme – death – that was always to dominate his work. Two scholarships enabled him to visit France, where he became interested in the Pont-Aven group and was influenced for a time by Gauguin, Van Gogh and Seurat. In Germany, on the 5th November 1892, he showed a part of his 'Frise de la Vie" ("Life's Frieze") on the occasion of the creation of the Secession of Berlin, and this picture caused such a scandal that the exhibition was closed the day after its opening. His influence has remained considerable in Germany, where he left a deep mark on Expressionism.

NITTIS, GIUSEPPE DE

Born at Barletta 22nd February 1846. Died at Saint-Germain-en-Laye (Seine-et-Oise) 24th August 1884. He went to Paris in 1868, worked in Gérôme's studio and made his debut at the Salon of 1869 with "The Woman with a Parrot" and "Intimate Reception". He had a rapid success and later an agreeable stay in England. His brilliant art was well suited to the seductive subjects that he treated –

streets in Paris or London, elegant young women, scenes of wordly life.

PISSARRO, CAMILLE

Born in St. Thomas (a Danish island in the Antilles) 10th July 1830. Died in Paris 13th November 1903. At the age of twelve, Camille Pissarro was sent to study in Paris. His father, a French Jew of Portuguese origin who had a business in a Danish island in the Antilles, thought the boy was developing a preference for commerce rather than drawing, for which he had already shown some leaning. When the young Pissarro returned in 1847 he felt so ill at ease in the family business that, some years later, in 1852, he left for Caracas with the Danish painter, Fritz Malbye. At this, his father sent him back to Paris in 1855 to study painting. In 1857 Pissarro met Monet at the Swiss Academy. A great admirer of Corot, he painted landscapes and exhibited several times at the Salon; but its doors were shut to him in 1863 and so he took part in the Salon des Refusés. In 1871 he went to London, where he met Monet and Durand-Ruel again. When he returned to France he found his home in Louveciennes sacked by the Germans and all his pictures destroyed. He was wholly attached to the Impressionist movement, and was to know years of great poverty, all the heavier to bear because he had a large family to support. In 1885 he met Seurat through Signac and, in 1886, adopted the principles of Neo-Impressionism – a short-lived experiment. He was to return to Impressionism some years later, around 1890. Most of Pissarro's pictures were painted at Louveciennes, Pontoise and, later, at Eragny-sur-Epte, where the artist settled in 1884.

We are indebted to him, moreover, for an important series on Rouen and another on Paris; when his tired eyes would no longer let him work in the open in winter, he would install himself in some Paris hotel and paint those views overlooking the bridges, the Avenue de l'Opéra and the Tuileries gardens, which are among the most vivid urban images that Impressionism has left us. Although some years older than the other painters in the group, Pissarro did not start tasting success until around 1890. He was almost sixty! The years of poverty had been long.

PUVIS DE CHAVANNES, PIERRE

Born in Lyons 14th December 1824. Died in Paris 24th October 1898. The creator of a form of Classicism that nevertheless appeared bold in his time, Puvis de Chavannes deserves to be considered one of the greatest decorators of his period. He introduced a very personal element into mural decoration through his way of treating landscape, through the long static forms of his characters and through the calm of his pictures. Less influenced by Impressionism than one might imagine, he acquired his taste for fresh colours more from the primitive painters of frescoes.

He exhibited for the first time at the Salon of 1850.

RAVIER, AUGUSTE-FRANCOIS

Born in Lyons 4th May 1814. Died at Morestel (Isère) 26th June 1895. He was haunted by light, which he rendered more as a poet than as a painter; he often resembled Turner, but his work has a more despairing tone. His landscapes have a fairy light. After having lived in Lyons, Italy and Loire, he spent the last 32 years of his life in Morestel.

REDON, ODILON

Born in Bordeaux 22nd April 1840. Died in Paris 6th July 1916. To use his own expression, he wanted to make his art "a little door opening on to mystery". In order to create the individual style that was to enable him to express his visions, in which the seen and the felt are mingled, he became a passionate observer of plants and animals; in order to uncover their personality, to put it on a level with humanity, he even went as far as taking lessons with the botanist, Clavand, at the same time that he was studying with Gérôme. All this science and technical virtuosity did not produce a barren, insipid result in him; on the contrary, they made the dream more profound. He said so himself: "In art, nothing is done by will alone. Everything is done by docile submission to what comes from the unconscious". So it is not surprising that the Symbolist writers found an illustration of their ideas in his work. He had begun with etchings; his first book of lithographs appeared in 1879. But he had to wait until 1899 before an important exhibition, at Durand-Ruel's Gallery, brought him really out of his isolation. He was always to reject the narrow outlook of a "School", found the Impressionists "rather unimaginative" and in his art always gave the predominant role to the imagination.

RENOIR, PIERRE-AUGUSTE

Born at Limoges 25th February 1841. Died at Cagnes 3rd December 1919. The story of Renoir's life would deserve to be the subject of an Epinal picture, with its toil, its predestination, its strife, its disappointments and success. He lived long and had many children.

Born into a family of modest means, and even poor, it is said, he became apprenticed to a porcelain-maker in Paris (rue du Temple) in 1854, and his early bent for drawing gave promise that he would be a good decorator. Having learnt to make bouquets of flowers, he then became a painter of fans, ornaments, sacred subjects, and screens destined for religious purposes. The good worker having thus saved some money, he was able to pay for some real lessons from real artists and, in 1862, enter Gleyre's studio, where he met Monet, Sisley and Bazille. During the same period, he made the acquaintance of Pissarro and Cézanne, who were both going to the Swiss Academy. Thus, well before the 1874 Exhibition the Impressionist team was made up. Renoir's pictures were severely criticised at the time of the first exhibition, yet he was one of the first to know the collectors' confidence, notably that of Georges Charpentier who, having bought one of his canvasses at the sale held in 1875, from the following year onwards gave him commissions to paint portraits of his family.

One is astonished today that works like "La Loge" (1874) and "le Moulin de la Galette" (1876) did not immediately gain the public's unanimous approval. By 1880 Renoir had almost won the day. From then on he was regularly received at the Salon and had small inclination for revolutionary movements. In 1881 he left for Italy, and returned in 1882; during these travels, Raphael exerted a strong influence on him which was to last for several years and drove him to adopt a more precise style of drawing, accentuating the outline of forms. This has been called his Ingres period because, renouncing the Impressionist play of colours, like Ingres he modelled his figures by blending colours and not by contrasting them. He protracted this experiment until around 1890, and then without turning back to Impressionist techniques, he found a freer way of painting in which his temperament expressed itself unrestrainedly. To his last day, Renoir's happy art was to give no indication of the physical suffering of a man rendered more and more paralytic by rheumatism. His children, his wife and especially his servant, Gabrielle, served him as models, in addition to flowers and Mediterranean landscapes, particularly those in the vicinity of Cagnes, where he settled in 1903 and where he spent most of his remaining years.

ROLL, ALFRED-PHILIPPE

Born in Paris 10th March 1847. Died there 27th October 1919. Before entering l'Ecole des Beaux-Arts where he was a pupil of Bonnat, Harpignies and Gérôme, he was a designer of ornaments. He travelled in Holland, Germany and Belgium. His work, dominated by the social questions of the day, carries the stamp of Zola rather than that of Courbet. He was one of the founders of the Société Nationale des Beaux-Arts.

ROSSETTI, GABRIEL-CHARLES-DANTE ("Dante-Gabriel-Rossetti")

Born in London 12th May 1828. Died at Birchington-on-Sea 9th April 1882. At the age of nineteen, when he was already known as a poet, he decided to devote himself to painting but, disheartened by Classical teaching and anxious to realise a lofty ideal, he teamed up with Holman Hunt and Millais in 1849 in order to found the Pre-Raphaelite Brotherhood, which was to have a profound influence on English painting.

ROUSSEAU, ETIENNE-PIERRE-THÉODORE

Born in Paris 15th April 1812. Died at Barbizon 22nd December 1867. At the age of eighteen, he abandoned all teaching to travel and to paint according to Nature. In 1832 (he was twenty) his style was similar to those of Constable and Bonington, but he used light in a way that resembled methods of the Dutch. He led a dignified life but difficult, success only coming his way after 1855. He is considered the leader of the Barbizon School.

RYDER, ALBERT PINKHAM

Born at New Bedford (Massachusetts) 19th March 1847. Died in Long Island (New York) 28th March 1917. He often worked in the greatest disorder and with no method (it is said that he went so far as using the wood of his bed if he was without canvas). Among his most famous pictures are « The Sea-Workers" and "Cove in the Moonlight", which are in New York and Washington. He also wrote lyrical poetry in which one finds the same poetic, almost romantic, sentiment that he brought to his painting, notably in the evocation of the sea.

Pierre-Auguste Renoir
Two Laundresses
1889
Private Collection
Paris

RYSSELBERGHE, THÉODORE or THÉO VAN

Born at Gand 28th November 1862. Died at Saint-Clair (Var) 13th December 1926. After Classical studies at Gand and Brussels he began painting thick and dark, but after a trip to Morocco, from where he brought back "La Fantasia" (1884) which was painted in luminous colours, he went to Paris, met Seurat and embraced Divisionism; he was to remain faithful to the Divisionist brush-stroke until 1910. In 1895 he contributed to the rebirth of decorative art in Belgium by designing furniture, ornaments and posters. To the fore in the intellectual and artistic movements of his time, he was one of those responsible for the foundation of the XX Group. An important retrospective exhibition of his work took place in Brussels in 1927.

SAEDELEER, VALERIUS DE

Born at Alost 4th August 1867. Died at Leupegen in 1941. Until around 1904 one finds in his work a reflection of the restless, troubled life he led, dominated by its often violent social side. Later he painted calmer landscapes, reminiscent of Brueghel. He lived in Laethem-Saint-Martin from 1893 to 1898 and again from 1904 to 1918; it was during the second stay that he veered away from the Impressionist technique, and his art was to become more and more decorative during the years he spent in England (1914-1921). At Etinchove-les-Audenaerde, where he later settled, he even opened a workshop for carpets and fabrics.

SEGANTINI, GIOVANNI

Born at Arco (Lake Garda) 15th January 1858. Died near Pontresina (Upper Engadine) 28th September 1899. This painter's life was very colourful. A poor orphan from the age of four, he was working as a shepherd near Milan when a drawing he had scratched on the stone wall of a hut was noticed by a tourist who took an interest in the child and helped him to study drawing and painting.

At the age of nineteen, Segantini exhibited his first picture, wich was rather Classical in style. Without ever leaving Italy, he was influenced by the various artistic tendencies of his time; little by little he gave light to his palette and adopted the Divisionist technique which to him seemed better suited to mountain landscapes, his favourite subject. And it was when painting a snowy landscape at Sovogino that he caught cold and died within a few days.

SÉRUSIER, LOUIS-PAUL-HENRI

Born in Paris in 1865. Died at Morlaix 6th October 1927. He was one of the first to recognise Gauguin's genius and proclaimed it to the group of young painters who attended Doucet's studio (where he was treasurer) at the Julian Academy, Bonnard, Vuillard, Maurice Denis, Piot, Ibels, Roussel, Ranson. Having met Gauguin during a stay at Pont-Aven in 1888, he abandoned traditional art, to which he had devoted himself till then, in order to paint a picture, "The Talisman", according to the ideas of the master in reaction against Impressionism, a picture in which the new doctrine expresses itself with great intensity. This picture was like a symbol for the Nabis (the name that the young artists grouped round Sérusier had adopted). His work, which is not without poetry and sometimes has the strange charm of Mediaeval imagery, is however that of a theoretician conscious of the means of expression that he used and always concerned to serve an ideal. But one cannot deny the importance of his influence on the evolution of contemporary art.

SEURAT, GEORGES

Born in Paris 2nd December 1859. Died there 29th March 1891. Georges Seurat first took lessons with Léon Lehmann at l'Ecole des Beaux-Arts. His friends there were Ernest Laurent and Aman-Jean, on whom he had a great influence when, attracted by Impressionism, he sought a method by which he could use the technique of short separate strokes while keeping the strict design and Classical construction that the l'Ecole had taught him. Seurat created a method out of the instinctive discoveries of the Impressionists, drawing on the scientific theories of Chevreul, Edward Rood and Charles Henry concerning the decomposition of colours. Neither Aman-Jean nor Ernest Laurent could understand how much of Seurat's invention was really new; they were content to adopt the method without

adopting its spirit. It was in those from outside his group of intimate friends that Seurat found a keener understanding and an extension of his ideas, notably in Signac and Cross. With a number of others, he was to create the movement that constituted the logical development of Impressionism. But in pushing the principles propounded by Monet and his friends to an extreme, this movement, called "Divisionism" or "Neo-Impressionism", also revealed its ultimate possibilities, that is to say, its limits. In his passion for construction, Seurat was in fact the first to understand the necessity of reacting against the dispersal and fluidity of forms and it is entirely logical that the Cubists should have turned to his work.

SICKERT, WALTER RICHARD

Born in Munich 31st May 1860. Died at Bath, England, 22nd January 1942. His family, artists of Danish origin, settled in England when he was nine and it was in that country that his artistic education began, at the Slade School. Later, he became a pupil and collaborator of Whistler's. Towards 1883 he went to Paris, teamed up with Degas and for a time was influenced by Impressionism. During his travels in France and Italy he adopted different themes, but his best period seems to have been that of his stay in Bath (1916-17) where he painted landscapes expressing every nuance of light and atmosphere. He became a teacher at the Royal Academy in London in 1926, and sacrificed his work somewhat to his duties.

SIGNAC, PAUL

Born in Paris 11th November 1863. Died there 15th August 1935. His family intended him to become an architect, but Signac showed a very early preference for painting and followed courses at the free academy of Bing. Very soon attracted by the art of the Impressionists, he became one of the adepts of Divisionism at the time of Seurat's first experiments and remained faithful to it till the end of his life. Through his and Pissarro's influence this technique figured among the last manifestations of Impressionism. Having played a part in the foundation of the Salon des Indépendants, in 1884, with Seurat, he became its president in 1908. Signac travelled a lot, but all his work is marked by his passionate love for the sea, which he surveyed more often from the yachts that he himself steered. One is indebted to him for views of Saint-Tropez,

Collioure, La Rochelle, Antibes, Genoa, Venice and Constantinople. He had a liking for sunny landscapes and luminous harmonies. After Seurat, he remains the painter thanks to whom Neo-Impressionism deserves a chosen place in the history of contemporary art.

SIGNORINI, TELEMACO

Born in Florence 18th August 1835. Died there 10th February 1901. He was one of the first painters of his generation to break with the traditionalist outlook. He had an acute, questing mind and was also an art critic and poet. Having made his debut in Florence in 1860 and exhibited in various Italian cities, he went to Paris in 1861 and met Corot and Troyon. At that time, he loved violent tone-contrasts, the light and the dark; the canvas that best represents this style is his "Sunny Day at La Spezia". After 1868, although he often let himself be led by his spirit rather than by his sensibility, his style became softer, he sought subtler, more subdued tonalities and his contrasts became less jarring.

SISLEY, ALFRED

Born in Paris 30th October 1839. Died at Moret 29th January 1899. We know little of Sisley's life and little has been written about his work. His parents, who were of English origin, intended him to go into commerce, but he preferred to enter Gleyre's studio (in 1862) where he met Bazille, Monet and Renoir, with whom he later stayed near Fontainebleau. He was protected from want by his family, and because of that was considered an amateur by his friends; but after the war, during which he was in England, he returned to Paris ruined and had to rely entirely on painting for a living. He was to know poverty until almost the end of his life, for success did not come so soon for him as for his friends and he died without knowing its benefit. After his death the situation changed: a sale of twenty-seven of his pictures fetched 12,320 francs (these proceeds going to his children), and the following year the canvas entiled "Flooding at Marly" brought the sum, enormous for those times, of 43,000 francs. If one excepts the few short stays he made in England and Normandy, all Sisley's life was spent, all his work done, in the region of Paris and Moret. He could render the quiet charm, the atmosphere quivering with light, of these places, and their gentle harmonies with their subtle poetry.

SLEVOGT, MAX

Born at Landshut 8th October 1868. Died at Neukastel 20th September 1932. Much influenced by Manet's art, a certain facility brought him quick success, and he pursued an untroubled career. A genre-painter and engraver, all he took from Impressionism was the liking for fresh, luminous colours, without adopting its disciplines.

SLUYTERS, JAN

Born at Bois-le-Duc 17th December 1881. Died in Amsterdam in 1957. Having studied with Allebé at the Amsterdam Academy, he was influenced by Impressionism and later became a Futurist, but carrying the mark of Gauguin. Towards 1913 he flirted with Cubism but soon returned to an art near that of Breitner. In 1904 he won a Prix de Rome, but in 1905 it was withdrawn because his teachers were dissatisfied with him. In 1907 he settled in Amsterdam.

TOOROP, JAN or JOHANNES THEODORUS

Born at Poerworedjo (Java) 20th December 1858. Died at La Hague in March 1928. He went to Holland around 1873, studied in Amsterdam, Brussels and later Paris, and travelled a lot. Between 1882 and 1885 he was influenced by Bastien-Lepage, Manet and Ensor but, towards 1890, he turned to Symbolism and became the most authentic representative of Neo-Impressionism in the Low Countries.

TOULOUSE-LAUTREC, HENRI DE

Born at Albi 24th November 1864. Died at the Château of Malromé 9th September 1901. All Toulouse-Lautrec's life and work were a kind of bravado, an acceptance of, and protest against, his fate. Born of a noble family, a lover of hunting and the gay life, he was dogged by misfortune from the days of his childhood. He fell down, broke his legs, became a cripple. Hideously ugly, and at odds with his family, he went to live in the company of street-girls, frequented public dances, dragged his pitiful infirmity and cruel compassion along the slippery paths of debauchery. One will never know whether he was aware of the admiration that he aroused or wounded by the disgust that he sometimes provoked. It is said that he was an historian of his time because he painted acid-cruel portraits of a number of ac-

tresses and dancers, but his observations only concerned a very limited world. However, within these limits, he shows such keen observation, his drawing is so incisive, that his art goes far beyond the anecdote it seems to recount. He followed in the Degas tradition, not only in his choice of subjects but also in some of the colours he used and his technique, perhaps also in the misanthropy with which, like Degas, he revealed but tried to hide, the soul of a disillusioned romantic.

TURNER, JOSEPH MALLORD WILLIAM

Born in London 23rd April 1775. Died there 19th December 1851. From the age of nine he made copies of engravings, which his father showed in the window of his barber shop, thereby attracting art-lovers. Dr. Monro taught him water-colour technique, after which he worked for an architect before entering the Royal Academy. In 1790 he exhibited for the first time; he was fifteen. From 1813 onwards he banished browns and blacks from his palette, but it was only after 1819 that he adopted the brilliant colours that were to inspire Monet.

VAN, GOGH VINCENT

Born at Groot-Zundert (Holland) 30th March 1853. Died at Auvers-sur-Oise 29th July 1890. It would be desirable not to write anything more on Van Gogh's life, so much has his material and moral degradation been unnecessarily laid out to view; one would like to see the public less curious about his tragic life and more interested in the wonderfully exultant spirit of his work. But it is difficult to separate one from the other, for if we deny ourselves the right to search, in the fireiest of Van Gogh's pictures, for a trace of mental derangement, it is no less true that the lyricism of his art stems from the intensity of his feelings, and perhaps it is not in vain that we examine the nature of these feelings for an explanation of their intensity. Thus, when taken up by an immense pity for humanity, and especially for the miners of Borinage, he tried to become a pastor and live like them in order to tend their souls better, his painting became harsh, the lines hard, the colours sombre. It was only in disillusionment, after the failures of his various experiments, it was only when humanity seemed to have completely rejected him, that he devoted himself exclusively to painting and found joy in brilliant, vibrant colours, in that ardent technique where every stroke of the brush is charged with passion. Van Gogh only arrived at this blossoming when all love had been refused him. The failures began early, perhaps even when, a rather wild child, he did not join in his friends' or his brothers' games. In London, where the adolescent had gone to gain experience, there was his landlord's daughter who did not wish to become his fiancée; then there were alternating reconciliations and breaks with his family which make it more and more difficult to understand his extraordinary character; there was his cousin, who refused to become his wife; there were other failures, about which we know little; there was even his attempt to save a prostitute. And this yearning for self-sacrifice always ended in bewilderment, loneliness, and even drama in the case of his friendship with Gauguin – a drama that ended in Arles in 1888 without costing the life of either of these artists, although Van Gogh cut off his ear with a razor to punish himself for having threatened his friend. Two years later, hope dead, with desperate, calm lucidity, Van Gogh put an end to his life by shooting himself with a revolver. His painting was an outlet for his fervour and it was from this turbulent art that Expressionism was to emerge later, like a liberation of Man from his neuroses.

VERNAY, FRANCOIS ("Francis Miel")

Born in Lyons in 1821. Died there in 1896. He remains one of the masters of the Lyons tradition in which still lifes are comprised of flowers and fruit. The richness of his colours, the harmonies he created, the variety he lent to one theme – these ensure him a special place among the many artists who have specialised in this genre.

Vincent van Gogh Landscape. Arles. c. 1888
Private Collection, Paris

VUILLARD, EDOUARD

Born at Cuiseaux (Saône-et-Loire) 11th November 1868. Died at La Baule (Loire Atlantique) 21st June 1940. Vuillard, whose long friendship with Pierre Bonnard and Roussel lasted till his dying day, like them had a life of conscientious toil, with no apparent scandal or strife. Like Bonnard, he made it his aim to paint an intimate picture of the bourgeoisie of his time, interiors with their velvety silence, lamps shedding a golden light on garments, bourgeois, drawing-rooms with their plush furniture and windows decked in tulle curtains. Like Bonnard, he had imbibed Gauguin's ideas at the Julian Academy, through Sérusier. Like Bonnard, he had belonged to the Nabis group, but little by little that fanciful creation of a number of young people faded into oblivion and it was only much later that, for the convenience of critics, it was given the title of "School". In an age when the great movements in painting often stemmed from agressive theories, Vuillard was guided by his sensibility, and his feelings as a painter grew tender before the spectacle of daily life; he expressed the charm of ordinary things.

WHISTLER, JAMES ABBOTT McNEIL

Born at Lowell (Massachusetts) 10th July 1834. Died in London 17th July 1903. Claimed by both the American and English Schools, most of his student days were spent in France; in particular, he worked in Gleyre's studio with Degas, Fantin-Latour, etc. In 1860 he settled in London, where he was known principally as a portraitist and where, for several years, he played a useful role in the evolution of artistic taste by making known the work of his French Impressionist friends.

WILLUMSEN, JENS-FERDINAND

Born in Copenhagen 7th September 1863. Died in Cannes 4th April 1958. He went to France for the first time in 1888, and met Gauguin at Pont-Aven in 1890. An engraver, architect, sculptor, painter and ceramist, he was employed by a porcelain factory between 1897 and 1900. He was one of the first sculptors to adopt the decorative style.

WOESTYNE, GUSTAVE VAN DE

Born at Gand 2nd August 1881. Died in Brussels in 1947. One of the first to settle in Laethem-St. Martin, with his brother Karel, the poet. He was profoundly influenced by George Minne and De Saedeleer. He very resolutely opposed Impressionism with his gaunt style, his hard lines and almost abstract designs, his cold, acid colours which often lack harmony, and his meticulous technique.

WOUTERS, RIK

Born at Malines 21st August 1882. Died in Amsterdam 11th July 1916. He studied painting and sculpture at Malines and in Brussels. His artistic career lasted for only seven years. His work is a synthesis of two opposing influences – on the one hand, that of Ensor which fired him to express himself in fluid, transparent colours, and on the other, that of Cézanne which whetted his feeling for structural composition. He remains the supreme master of Brabantine Fauvism.

ZANDOMENEGHI, FEDERICO

Born in Venice 2nd June 1841. Died in Paris 30th December 1917. His father and grandfather were sculptors. He first studied with his father and then, after a number of years in Florence and Venice, he went to Paris in 1874 and immediately joined the Impressionist movement. He exhibited at the Salon des Indépendants.

BIBLIOGRAPHY

GENERAL SOURCES

Adhémar, H. and Dayez, A.   Musée de l'impressionnisme. Paris 1973

Alazard, J.   L'Orient et la peinture française au dix-neuvième siècle. D'Eugène Delacroix à Auguste Renoir. Paris 1930

Barnes, A. C.   The Art in Painting. New York 1925

Basler, A. and Kunstler, Ch.   La peinture indépendante en France. Paris 1929

Basler, A.   Modern French Painting: the Post-Impressionists from Monet to Bonnard. New York 1931

Bazin, G.   L'époque impressionniste. Paris 1947

Bazin, G.   French Impressionists in the Louvre. New York 1958

Bell, Clive   Since Cézanne. London 1922

Bell, Clive   An Account of French Painting. New York 1932

Besson, G.   L'impressionnisme et quelques précurseurs. Paris 1932

Blanche, J.-E.   Propos de peintre. De David à Degas. Première série: Ingres, David, Manet, Degas, Renoir, Cézanne, Whistler, Fantin-Latour, Ricard, Couder, Beardsley, etc. Preface by Marcel Proust. Paris 1919

Blunden, M. and G.   Impressionists and Impressionism. New York 1970

Boime, Albert   The Academy and French Painting in the Ninenteenth Century. London – New York 1971

Bouret, J.   The Barbizon School and Nineteenth Century French Landscape Painting. London 1973

Bowness, Alan ed.   Impressionists and Post-Impressionists. New York 1965

Cassou, J.   Die Impressionisten und ihre Zeit. Munich

Castagnary   Salons de 1857 à 1879. Paris 1892

Champa, Kermit Swiler.   Studies in Early Impressionism. New Haven 1973

Chu, P.   French Realism and the Dutch Masters. Utrecht 1974

Clay, J. ed.   Impressionism. Preface by René Huyghe. New York 1973

Cogniat, R.   French Painting at the Time of the Impressionists. New York 1951

Cogniat, R.   Histoire de la peinture. Paris 1955

Cogniat, R., Elgar, F., Selz, J.   Dictionnaire de l'impressionnisme. Paris

Courthion, Pierre.   Autour de l'impressionnisme. Paris 1964

Courthion, Pierre.   Impressionism. New York 1972

Denis, M.   Théories 1890-1910. Du symbolisme et de Gauguin vers un nouvel ordre classique. Paris 1912

Denvir, B.   Impressionism. London 1974

Desnoyers, F.   Le Salon des refusés. La peinture en 1863. Paris 1863

Dewhurst, W.   Impressionist Painting. London 1904

Dorival, B.   Les étapes de la peinture française contemporaine, tome I : de l'impressionnisme au fauvisme. Paris 1945

Dorival, B.   Histoire de l'art. Encyclopédie de la Pléiade. Paris 1969

Duranty, L.   Réalisme. Paris 1856-57

Duranty, L.   La nouvelle peinture. A propos du groupe d'artistes qui expose dans les Galeries Durand-Ruel. Paris 1876; reprint 1946

Duret, Th.   Le peintre français en 1867. Paris o.J.

Duret, Th.   Les peintres impressionnistes. Paris 1878

Duret, Th.   Critique d'avant-garde. Paris 1885

Duret, Th.   Les maîtres impressionnistes. Paris 1900

Duret, Th.   Histoire des peintres impressionnistes. Paris 1906

Duret, Th.   Manet and the French Impressionists. Philadelphia – London 1970

Duret, Th.   Die Impressionisten. 5th ed. Berlin 1923

Faure, E.   History of Art. Modern Art. New York 1924

Fénéon   Les impressionnistes en 1886. Paris 1886

Fèvre, H.   Etude sur le Salon de 1886 et sur l'Exposition des impressionnistes. Paris 1886

Focillon, H.   La peinture au XIXe et XXe siècles. Du réalisme à nos jours. Paris 1928

Francastel, P.   L'impressionnisme. Les origines de la peinture moderne, de Monet à Gauguin. Paris 1937

Francastel, P.   History of French Painting, v. II : From Classicism to Cubism. Amsterdam – New York 1955

Francastel, P.   La réalité figurative. Paris 1965

Fry, R.   Transformations. London 1926

Gaunt, W.   Impressionism. A Visual History. New York 1970

Gauss, C. E.   The Aesthetic Theories of French Artists, 1855 to the Present. Baltimore 1949

Geffroy, G.   Histoire de l'impressionnisme. Paris

Gibson, F.   Six French Artists of the Nineteenth Century. London 1925

Gràber, H.   Camille Pissarro, Alfred Sisley, Claude Monet nach eigenen und fremden Zeugnissen. 1943

Hammann, R.   Der Impressionismus in Leben und Kunst. Marburg 1923

Handbuch der Kunstwissenschaft.   Malerei des 19. Jahrhunderts. Potsdam 1913-30

Hartlaub, G. F.   Die Impressionisten in Frankreich. Wiesbaden 1936

Hautecoeur, L.   Histoire de l'art. Paris 1959

Heilbut, E.   Die Impressionisten. Berlin 1903

Herbert, R. L.   Neo-Impressionism. New York 1968

Homer, W.   Seurat and the Science of Painting. Cambridge, Mass. 1964

Huneker, J. G.   Promenades of an Impressionist. New York 1910

Huyghe, R.   La relève du réel. Paris 1974

Huysmans, J.-K.   Certains. Paris 1889

Huysmans, J.-K.   L'art moderne. Paris 1908. Reprint Farnborough 1969

Jamot, P.   La peinture en France. Paris 1934

Jaworska, W.   Gauguin et l'école de Pont-Aven, Neuchâtel 1971

Jewell, E. A.   French Impressionists and their Contemporaries. New York 1946

Klein, J.   Modern Masters. New York 1938

Landsberger, Fr.   Impressionismus und Expressionismus. Eine Einführung in das Wesen der neuen Kunst. Leipzig 1922

Laprade, J.   L'impressionnisme. Paris 1956

Lassaigne, J.   Impressionism. New York 1969

Lassaigne, J.   La grande histoire de la peinture. Geneva 1974

Lazar, Béla   Die Maler des Impressionismus (6 Vorträge). Leipzig – Berlin 1919

Lecomte, G.   L'art impressionniste d'après la collection privée de M. Durand-Ruel. Paris 1892

Lemoyne de Forges, M.-T.   Barbizon et l'école de Barbizon. Paris 1971

Leymarie, J.   Impressionism. Lausanne 1955-59

Leymarie, J.   Impressionists. Drawings from Manet to Renoir. Geneva 1969

Leymarie, J. and Melot, M.   Les gravures des impressionnistes – Oeuvre complet. Paris 1971

Leroy, A.   Histoire de la peinture française 1800-1933. Paris 1934

Løvgren   The Genesis of Modernism. Seurat, Gauguin, Van Gogh and French Symbolism in the 1880s. Stockholm 1959. A University of Uppsala Thesis.

Mallet, J. W.   The Barbizon Painters. London 1890

Marumo, C.   Barbizon et les paysagistes du XIXᵉ. Paris 1975

Mathey, F.   The Impressionists. New York 1961-1967

Mauclair, C.   The French Impressionists. New York 1903, London 1911

Mauclair, C.   Les états de la peinture française de 1850 à 1920. Paris 1921

Mauclair, C.   L'impressionnisme. Son histoire, son esthétique, ses maîtres. Paris 1923

Maus, M.-O.   Trente années de lutte pour l'Art. Bruxelles 1926

Meier-Graefe, J.   Impressionisten. Munich 1907

Meier-Graefe, J.   Entwicklungsgeschichte der moderne Kunst. 2 Aufl. Munich 1927

Miscellaneous Authors.   Nouveau dictionnaire de la peinture moderne. Paris 1963

Miscellaneous Authors.   Catalogue of Exhibition « Impressionism : A Centenary Exhibition ». New York, Metropolitan Museum of Art. December 1974 - February 1975

Moore, G.   Confessions of a Young Man. London 1888

Moore, G.   Modern Painting. New York 1906

Moore, G.   Reminiscences of the Impressionist Painters. Dublin 1906

Musée de l'Orangerie.   Impressionnistes et romantiques français dans les musées allemands. Catalogue. Paris 1951

Muther, R.   Ein Jahrhundert französicher Malerei. Berlin 1901

Muther, R.   The History of Modern Painting. London 1907

Novotny, Fr.   Painting and Sculpture in Europe - 1780 to 1880. London 1960

Palluchini, R.   Gli Impressionisti alla XXIV Biennale di Venezia. Preface by L. Venturi. Venice 1948

Pica, V.   Gli Impressionisti Francesi. Bergamo 1908

Picard, M.   Das Ende des Impressionismus. Munich 1916

Picon, G.   1863 : Naissance de la peinture moderne. Geneva 1974

Pillement, G.   Les pré-impressionnistes. Paris 1974

Pool, P.   Impressionism. New York - London 1967

Poulain, G.   Bazille et ses amis. Paris 1932

Ragghianti, C. L.   Impressionismo. Torino 1944

Raphael, M.   Von Monet zu Picasso. Munich 1919

Raynal, M.   Histoire de la peinture moderne, de Baudelaire à Bonnard. Geneva 1950

Raynal, M.   De Goya à Gauguin. Geneva 1951

Rewald, J.   Post-Impressionism from Van Gogh to Gauguin, 2nd ed. New York 1962

Rewald, J.   The History of Impressionism, 4th rev. ed. New York 1973

Rey, R.   La peinture française à la fin du XIXᵉ siècle. La renaissance du sentiment classique. Paris 1931

Roger-Marx, Cl.   Un siècle d'art. Paris 1904

Roger-Marx, Cl.   Les impressionnistes. Paris 1956

Roskill, M.   Van Gogh, Gauguin and the Impressionist Circle. Greenwich, Conn. 1970

Rothenstein, J.   Nineteenth Century Painting. London 1932

Salmon, A.   Propos d'atelier. Paris 1922

Scharf, A.   Art and Photography. London 1968

Scheffler, K.   Die großen französichen Maler des 19. Jahrhunderts. Munich 1942

Schmidt, K. E.   Französiche Malerei des 19. Jahrhunderts. Leipzig 1903

Schneider, R.   L'art français aux XIXᵉ et XXᵉ siècles. Du réalisme à notre temps. Paris 1930

Seiberling, F.   Impressionism and its Roots. Iowa City, University of Iowa, Gallery of Art 1964

Serullaz, M.   The Impressionist Painters : French Painting. New York 1960

Serullaz, M., Pillement, G., Marret, B., Duret-Robert, F.   Encyclopédie de l'impressionnisme. Paris 1974

Signac, P.   D'Eugène Delacroix au néo-impressionnisme. Paris 1939

Sloane, J. C.   French Painting Between the Past and the Present; Artists, Critics and Tradition from 1848 to 1870. Princeton 1951

Slocombe, G.   Rebels of Art : Manet to Matisse. New York 1939

Sterling, C.   Great French Painting in the Hermitage. New York 1939

Stix, A.   Von Ingres bis Cézanne. 32 Handzeichnungen französicher Meister des 19. Jahrhunderts aus der Albertina. Vienna 1927

Sutter, J.   Les néo-impressionnistes. Lausanne – Neuchâtel 1970

Tabarant, A.   Le cinquantenaire de l'impressionnisme. La renaissance de l'art français. Paris 1924

Taylor, B.   The Impressionists and their World. London 1953

Uhde, W.   The Impressionists. New York 1937

University of California at Davis.   Pre-Impressionism, 1860-1869. Catalogue of Exhibition 1969

Venturi, L.   L'Impressionismo (« L'Arte », Nuova Serie 6) 1935

Venturi, L.   Impressionism. Art in America. New York 1936

Venturi, L.   Les archives de l'impressionnisme. Paris 1939

Venturi, L.   Impressionists and Symbolists. New York 1950

Vollard, A.   Souvenirs d'un marchand de tableaux de Meissonnier à Picasso. Paris

Waldmann, E. Die Kunst des Realismus und des Impressionismus im 19. Jahrhundert. Propylaen-Kunstgeschichte Band XV. Berlin 1927

Warnod, A. Bals, cafés et cabarets. Paris 1914

Weisbach, W. Impressionismus, Problem der Malerei in der Antike und Neuzeit. Berlin 1910-1911

Westheim, P. Helden und Abenteurer, Welt und Leben der Künstler. Berlin 1931

Wildenstein Galleries. One Hundred Years of Impressionism : A Tribute to Durand-Ruel. Catalogue of Exhibition. New York 1970

Wilenski, R. H. Modern French Painters. New York 1947

Wright, W. H. Modern Painting. Its Tendency and Meaning. London – New York 1915

Zola, E. Mon salon. Manet. Ecrits sur l'art. Paris 1970

Zola, E. Le bon combat : de Courbet aux impressionnistes. Paris 1974

Numerous books have been written on Impressionism. We have only mentioned here the most important works or the most recent ones.

It is impossible to list all the monographs devoted to the individual artists. We shall therefore limit this bibliography to the *catalogues raisonnés* :

BAZILLE
F. Daulte. Geneva 1952

BONNARD
Jean and Henri Dauberville. Paris 1965-74

BOUDIN
Robert Schmit. Paris 1973

CAILLEBOTTE
M. Berhaut. Paris 1951
(a *catalogue raisonné* is in preparation).

CASSATT
A. D. Breeskin. Washington 1970

CÉZANNE
L. Venturi. Paris 1936

DEGAS
P. A. Lemoisne. Paris 1946-1949

FANTIN-LATOUR
Mme Fantin-Latour. Paris 1911

GAUGUIN
G. Wildenstein & R. Cogniat. Paris 1964

GUILLAUMIN
G. Serret & D. Fabiani. Paris 1971

MANET
G. Wildenstein, P. Jamot & M. L. Bataille. Paris 1932

MANET
A. Tabarant. Paris 1947

MANET
D. Wildenstein & H. Rouart. Paris 1975

MONET
D. Wildenstein. Lausanne – Paris 1974

MORISOT
G. Wildenstein & M. L. Bataille. Paris 1961

PISSARRO
L. R. Pissarro & L. Venturi. Paris 1939

RENOIR
F. Daulte. Lausanne 1971

SEURAT
J. Rewald & H. Dorra. Paris 1960

SEURAT
C. M. de Hauke. Paris 1961

SISLEY
F. Daulte. Lausanne 1959

TOLOUSE-LAUTREC
M. G. Dortu. New York 1971

VAN GOGH
La Faille. New York 1938

MAGAZINE ARTICLES

Rivière, G. L'impressionniste. Journal d'Art, Paris 1877

Waern, C. Notes on French Impressionists. Atlantic Monthly, April 1892

Geffroy, G. L'impressionnisme. Revue encyclopédique, 15 December 1893

Goodrich, L. The Impressionists Fifty Years Ago. The Arts, January 1927

Poulain, G. Pré-Impressionnisme. Formes, November 1931

Rey, R. Les disciples de l'impressionnisme. « L'Amour de l'Art »

Huyghe, R. L'Impressionnisme et la pensée de son temps. Prométhée, February 1939

Huyghe, R. Genèse et position de l'art moderne. « L'Amour de l'Art ». Paris 1933

Venturi, L. The Aesthetic Idea of Impressionism. The Journal of Aesthetics, 1941

Scheyer, E. Far Eastern Art and French Impressionists, The Art, Quarterly, 1943

Venturi, L. Qu'est-ce que l'impressionnisme; Labyrinthe, 15. August 1944

Webster, J. C. The Technique of Impressionism. College Art Journal, November 1949

Bazin, G., Florisoone, M., Leymarie, J. Les impressionnistes. « L'Amour de l'Art ». Paris 1947

Reuterswald, O. The Accented Brush of the Impressionist. The Journal of Aesthetic and Art Criticism, March 1952

LIST OF ILLUSTRATIONS

CONTENTS